'Hitchhiking is the ultimate act of surrender and vulnerability where one must depend on the kindness of strangers and one's own inner patience. At a time of social and ecological transition, McKiernan opens himself to the road, offering up a moving window into the fears, dreams, and possibilities of the Irish land and people. More transporting than a travelogue, *Hitching for Hope* is a tale full of serendipitous encounters and the spirit of Ireland's byways.'

— CHUCK COLLINS, Institute for Policy Studies;
author of *Born on Third Base*

'Funny, philosophical, and moving, this book illuminates a lesser-seen map of a better and kinder humanity. In an age of cynicism and despair, the stories and insights Ruairí unveils are exactly the medicine we need to wake up and remember who we really are. Whether or not it persuades you to hitchhike to your next business meeting, this book will certainly remind you that people — and the future — may not be as scary as you thought.'

— AMANDA PALMER, singer-songwriter;
author of *The Art of Asking*

'Ruairí McKiernan hitchhikes through Ireland's soul — its heartbeat — to bring us an authentic and utterly compelling narrative. Think *McCarthy's Bar* for the socially conscious. An important and enjoyable read from a trusted voice.'

— BRIAN O'CONNELL, journalist;
author of *The Personals*

'Burnt out from his work as a community organizer, Ruairí McKiernan decided to hit the road. He stuck out his thumb — and his neck, too — hoping to learn something about himself and his country. A wholehearted testament to the power of deep listening and a beautiful glimpse into the Irish spirit, *Hitching for Hope* tells the story of his journey. There is cause for hope in these dark times, and Ruairí found it in the people.'

— ANDREW FORSTHOEFEL, author of *Walking to Listen*

PRAISE FOR *HITCHING FOR HOPE*

'In *Hitching for Hope*, Ruairí McKiernan sets out on a pilgrimage to capture truth and to hear stories that deserve to be heard. He sticks his thumb out, and somehow a healthy dose of humanity manages to roll up alongside him. McKiernan is a writer who finds home in the elsewhere. This book is a paean to nuance, decency and possibility.'

— COLUM MCCANN, author of *Let the Great World Spin*;
co-founder of Narrative 4

'Ruairí's tale of his journey comes as a breath of fresh air, awakening us to the adventures in store when we embark beyond well-trod routines into new encounters. It reminds me of my own hitchhiking trip in the UK seventy years ago — full of spunk, resilience, and zest for discovery. Whether "hitching for hope" or working together in a neighbourhood garden, we can link arms for the sake of the Great Turning to a life-sustaining future.'

— JOANNA MACY, author of *Coming Back to Life*

'Ruairí McKiernan takes time to look behind the stone walls of Ireland. Travelling from pillar to post, he takes note of what many of us some-times fail to see. Always revealing, always caring and compassionate.'

— CHRISTY MOORE, singer-songwriter

'The act of hitchhiking demands spontaneous interaction — a subversive moment of community between strangers that is increasingly lost or avoided in lives dictated by algorithms and automated route planners. The insights Ruairí McKiernan shares from people he meets on these freewheeling journeys somehow defy cynicism. The many voices in this book, from undocumented immigrants to young farmers, capture Ireland at a time of deep crisis but also radical change.'

— CAELAINN HOGAN, author of *Republic of Shame*

'Ireland went through its Celtic Tiger phase, all consumerism and growth. And then it crashed. In the aftermath, Ruairí McKiernan found that, like humans everywhere, what people really yearned for was community and connection, even if they'd almost forgotten how any of that worked. This is a tale that will resonate all over the world.'
— BILL MCKIBBEN, author of *Wandering Home*

'Making a reader stop and think is something we should all want to achieve, and Ruairí McKiernan succeeds. Ordinary people and their lived experiences are at the heart of this book. *Hitching for Hope* demonstrates that, despite a diversity of backgrounds, we all want the same things: to find peace and to help our families and communities flourish.'
— LYNN RUANE, Independent Senator; activist; author of *People Like Me*

'After travelling around Ireland and listening rather than speaking, McKiernan has produced a personal diary, a guided tour of his native country and an Irish *Canterbury Tales* for the twenty-first century. *Hitching for Hope* is a package of hope itself, full of kindness, political observations and of course the *craic*. Irish at its core and international in its search for optimism and communal involvement, it's an easy and uplifting read.'
— PEGGY SEEGER, singer-songwriter; author of *First Time Ever*

'In this pilgrimage around modern Ireland, Ruairí takes us to the people — to the nation's beating heart. At times we glimpse the light that, since the old Dark Ages, has been Ireland's gift to a hungry world.'
— ALASTAIR MCINTOSH, author of *Soil and Soul* and *Poacher's Pilgrimage*

'Listening requires focus, attention, and awareness — skills that Ruairí has perfected. He listens to so many different perspectives without reacting or debating, and opens his mind and heart to each of them. I highly recommend this book. I guarantee that you will not be able to put it down.'
— FRANCES BLACK, Independent Senator; singer; founder of RISE Foundation

Hitching for Hope

Hitching for Hope

A Journey into the Heart and Soul of Ireland

RUAIRÍ MCKIERNAN

CHELSEA GREEN PUBLISHING
White River Junction, Vermont
London, UK

Acquisitions Editor: Jon Rae
Developmental Editor: Natalie Wallace
Project Editor: Michael Metivier
Project Manager: Sarah Kovach
Copy Editors: Sarah Ingle and Jo Mortimer
Proofreader: Laura Jorstad
Indexer: Peggy Holloway
Designer: Melissa Jacobson

Printed in the United Kingdom.
First printing March 2020.
10 9 8 7 6 5 4 3 2   20 21 22 23

Library of Congress Cataloging-in-Publication Data
Names: McKiernan, Ruairí, author.
Title: Hitching for hope : a journey into the heart and soul of Ireland / Ruairí McKiernan.
Description: White River Junction, Vermont : Chelsea Green Publishing, [2020] | Includes index.
Identifiers: LCCN 2019049685 (print) | LCCN 2019049686 (ebook) |
   ISBN 9781603589574 (paperback) | ISBN 9781603589581 (ebook)
Subjects: LCSH: McKiernan, Ruairí — Travel — Ireland. | Ireland--Social conditions — 1973- |
   Ireland — Politics and government — 1949- | Ireland — History — 21st century.
Classification: LCC HN400.3.A8 M345 2020 (print) | LCC HN400.3.A8 (ebook)
   | DDC 306.09415 — dc23
LC record available at https://lccn.loc.gov/2019049685
LC ebook record available at https://lccn.loc.gov/2019049686

Chelsea Green Publishing
85 North Main Street, Suite 120
White River Junction, VT 05001

Somerset House
London, UK

www.chelseagreen.com

This book is dedicated to you, the reader,
for wherever you may need more hope in your life.

CONTENTS

PREFACE

When the call to adventure comes, it doesn't always make sense. It doesn't really need to. Sometimes you just have to take a leap of faith – to jump in and trust that things are going to work out.

Hitchhiking teaches you this. It leaves you at the side of the road, thumb to the wind, not knowing who might stop, where they might be going and what conversations might follow. When you're hitching, you either let go of your plans and go with the flow, or risk frustration and impatience over that which is outside your control. In many ways it's about surrendering to the path ahead.

I never envisioned writing a book, just as I never imagined I would hitchhike around Ireland. Even after my hitching trip, I didn't plan to write one. Yet this book seemed to have a life of its own; the call to write it persisted until I eventually relented.

Perhaps that's because ultimately, this isn't just my story to share. It is the story of so many people in Ireland, and so many across the world. The story of people trying to make sense of life, to hold on and to have hope during troubled times.

I have tried to capture the experiences of this trip as accurately as possible, working often from my notes and recordings. I also spent ages trying to track down all the people in the book (an adventure in itself!) to ensure they were happy to be mentioned. In a few instances I have changed names and certain details. Some conversations have been reconstructed from memory; in these cases, the quotations do not read verbatim. I have, however, worked hard to respect and honour all the people, places and stories I recount and hope that I have done them justice.

Hitching for Hope is an invitation to join me on the journey, and as you do, to reflect on your own story, your hopes and dreams and your role in helping to build a better world for all.

Ruairí McKiernan

RUAIRÍ'S ROUTE

Prologue

'HITCHING FOR HOPE? YOU'RE MESSING WITH ME. What on earth do you think that's going to achieve?' a well-dressed older man asked in the early days of my trip. He looked at me with a mixture of scorn, disbelief and amusement.

'No, I'm serious,' I replied calmly. 'Look, I've no idea if this will achieve anything. It's an experiment of sorts; just an idea that I feel is worth trying. It's a personal journey but hopefully it will come up with some answers to bigger questions. Time will tell.' I felt a little vulnerable under his spotlight, but accepted he had every right to be cynical and sceptical.

'Spare us all your hippy hope nonsense,' read a message I received on social media sometime after that. 'All this talk about hope is a distraction from the real work and radical change that we need to get on with. Get back to work!' it bluntly concluded. Ouch.

Matters of hope, happiness and vision for Ireland weren't going to be resolved through a brief solo hitching trip lacking in any great academic depth; that much was for sure. This was an amateur adventure, and I was fine with that. I wasn't setting out to impress, inspire or prove a point, but rather to listen. My heart was open and I would try to keep an open mind. After all, that's how I hoped to be received by others.

———

Back in 2013, I was feeling lost and frustrated, falling into a depression I couldn't understand. In the eyes of the world, I had so much going for me: I was engaged to be married to a wonderful woman, I had opportunities and options to consider, and I was in pretty good health. Yet something was missing.

Ireland, too, was in the eye of a tornado. It had been five years since one of the world's most dramatic economic collapses, and every day brought news of fresh scandals: abuses of power by bankers, politicians and the clergy. The downward spiral seemed relentless. People who had committed economic crimes walked away with apparent impunity. Former national leaders joined corporate boards, leaving the younger generation to supplement their generous pensions. Despite promises of reform, it appeared the prevailing order would merely march forward in different clothes.

Tens of thousands of young people were emigrating, unemployment was stuck at 15 per cent, and charities were struggling to keep their doors open. A new culture of unpaid internships emerged, bolstered by the logic that unpaid work would provide valuable experience and connections. There was some truth in that perhaps, but it wasn't everyone who could afford to work for free. In this climate it was hard not to become angry and bitter and let frustration turn to despair. Those who took to the streets were often vilified and warned not to threaten the country's stability, while at the same time certain commentators lamented a lack of civic action. Many people were retreating into themselves, losing hope and suffering feelings of resignation. Meanwhile, political leaders perpetuated a sense of shame, encouraging the belief that the crash was a collective responsibility rather than a systemic failure. 'We all partied' – that was their mantra, in reference to the boom years before the crash. Yet it seemed as if those who partied particularly hard were enabled by a kind of upside-down welfare system paid for by taxpayers through massive budget cuts to hospitals, schools and youth projects.

The chaos did not arise from a vacuum. From the mid-1990s until the late 2000s, a flood of cheap bank credit and foreign investment led to the beginning of what became known as Ireland's 'Celtic Tiger' economy. During this period, the country rapidly shifted from one of Europe's poorest to one of its wealthiest. New roads, restaurants, shopping centres and apartment complexes appeared almost overnight, in a dizzying burst of high-octane development that some in the media and politics portrayed as unstoppable. There was no denying the benefits – increased access to work, education and travel opportunities – but much of it was to be short-lived. A housing bubble lurked on the horizon, and when the US housing market collapsed in mid-2008, the writing was on the wall for Ireland. Our boom was about to go bust, and despite warnings from certain quarters, we weren't ready for it.

Following the collapse of the Irish economy, intense political and social upheaval rippled through communities, workplaces and families, leaving a trail of destruction in its wake. Poor leadership and crazy decisions, including the world's most expensive banking bailout, left Ireland one of the most indebted nations on the planet. It handed real power to the so-called Troika of the International Monetary Fund, the European Central Bank and the European Union. Ireland felt like a pale version of the country our ancestors must have dreamed of in their quest for independence only a century ago.

———

While the sharp decline and the Irish government's response evoked widespread anger, it also gave way to self-reflection. People started to ask bigger questions about the vision we were working towards as a society, and as individuals. *What kind of country are we living in? Where can hope be found? What is my role in it all?*

These questions hovered in my mind, too. In 2004, I had partnered with friends to establish an organisation called Community Creations, which in turn gave rise to SpunOut.ie, a pioneering youth movement that harnessed the internet to focus on issues including mental and sexual health as well as political empowerment. The organisation took off: we raised millions of euros, won numerous awards and helped organise a visit by the Dalai Lama to Ireland. Like Ireland's economy had been, I was flying high, propelled by adrenaline and a particular definition of success. However, just as the country had experienced a crash landing, I was about to endure my own.

By mid-2011, I had reached a point of burnout. There was no fuel left in the tank, and everything seemed to take more energy than it should. In some ways, I felt paralysed by fear and uncertainty, and I knew something needed to change.

Reading the Dalai Lama's writings, I took inspiration from his thoughts on how fear can infect our lives and limit our choices, and how by learning to live 'in the now' we might find greater peace. I began taking walks to determine what path I should take, with two perspectives competing for attention. One was at the heart level, what some call intuition, or gut instinct. It was telling me that I knew what I needed to do: to jump into the unknown. The other, originating in the rational part of the brain that craves logic and safety, was screaming at me to be clever and not throw everything away. There were other voices, too, including that of our modern society, which tells us to put material comfort above everything else and block out that internal voice that says, *I can't go on like this.*

I took a few weeks out to travel and reflect on the situation. Would I continue on, pushing for cultural change and better policies in the areas of health and well-being, while feeling confused and exhausted myself? If so, I concluded, I'd be a hypocrite and a fraud, not living the values I promoted. It was time to jump.

Within months, I had walked away from Community Creations entirely, giving the new leadership space to take the reins. I had given everything to establish this organisation, but now I needed to let go.

There is a saying, popular among optimists: 'Jump and the net will appear', but some time after jumping I still wasn't seeing any net. The recession was in full swing, work was slow to come in, I was falling into debt and there were no obvious next steps. I knew in my heart that leaving was the right decision, but that didn't stop my wobbles of doubt. Had I got it wrong?

I started to think about joining my many peers who were emigrating, but didn't want to leave with a bitter taste in my mouth. On the other hand, I needed to rediscover my zest for living and try to find some kind of peace with Ireland if I was to stay and build a life here with my then-fiancée, Susan. I needed to know if, beyond all the politics and promises, there really was hope for our country, and what my role might be.

———

I resolved to stay true to myself despite my worries and to keep pushing forward in the hope that something good would come eventually. Little did I know what was around the corner. 'Can you take a call from the President?' came a voice from the other end of the phone one day as I listened, slightly stunned. The newly elected President of Ireland, Michael D. Higgins, asked if I would accept an invitation to be one of his seven appointees to the Council of State, a Presidential advisory body of sorts. The other members of the Council were 'ex-officio' participants including the Taoiseach (Ireland's equivalent of Prime Minister), the Tánaiste (Deputy Prime Minister), and the Attorney General; former Presidents and Taosigh; and the President's seven appointees.

I had briefly met 'Michael D.', as he's affectionately known by many, two or three times before and had lobbied him during his candidacy to put youth issues on the national agenda. I had also read his book, *Causes for Concern*, and was impressed by his decades of campaigning for human and workers' rights, and by his championing of arts, culture and heritage issues. I was both shocked and honoured by the invitation. It was an unpaid role, but there wasn't a significant workload and it could enhance my ability to advocate as an independent community voice for change at the national level. The invitation felt like a message to 'keep going', a timely sign that I was on the right road, even if many things remained very uncertain. Burnout had taken a bigger toll than I realised, though. A year later, while I had made some progress, my usual energy levels had not returned. The political situation wasn't improving and I was finding it difficult to swallow the prospect of returning to a world of constant stress and busyness.

As I considered all of this, another life-changing opportunity came my way: an invitation to speak about citizens' views of Ireland at the MacGill summer school. On the surface, this was a straightforward speaking invite, but in reality it was an opportunity that would open a thousand doors. MacGill is a well-known forum for politicians, journalists and social commentators that takes place each summer in the village of Glenties, just north of the Bluestack Mountains in County Donegal. I had spoken there in the past, but over time had grown jaded; these types of events seemed to increasingly reinforce the same old stories from a limited range of perspectives. Besides, my confidence was low and I wasn't sure I had anything unique to say, much less the ability to inspire others. At the same time, I knew this was a chance to say things that needed to be aired. I felt a sense of responsibility to show up on behalf of the many who are never offered such a platform. Unsure of how to proceed, I ignored the invite for a few weeks.

Meanwhile, an idea was brewing, though I did not yet know what form it would take. My daily walks had brought me into contact with others who, like me, looked a little lost. Many had lost their jobs and were out walking as they tried to make sense of their lives. Together, we were looking for answers and desperate for change.

I wondered how I might use the MacGill invitation to do something different: to let people speak for themselves and to amplify their voices as best I could. That's when the idea of a listening project struck – a project I could use to hear real stories, understand common challenges and consider how we might maintain hope for the future during this time of darkness.

My first thought was to create some kind of online survey. While this sounded practical, it was missing the human dimension that I craved. I envisioned a more intimate form of interaction, one that would allow me to connect with people – to look into their eyes, and to hear their voices.

The next idea was to drive around Ireland, but I had recently sold my car and the cost of fuel and the carbon footprint impact would be significant. I sat on it for a while longer, tuning into the essence of what it was I was looking for; I knew I wanted to capture fresh truths in a raw, unplanned way, without the temptation to control where I might travel, who I might meet or what I might hear.

PROLOGUE

Hitchhiking! It's perfect! The idea came in a flash, alongside a cascade of memories from my teenage years on the road. A hitchhiking trip would satisfy the need for connection while simultaneously offering me a chance to shake things up and throw caution to the wind.

Against this backdrop I set forth on a journey to cultivate a deeper understanding of where hope might come from. Hope for myself, for Ireland and for humanity.

1

Roots and Uprooting

Spiddal

ONE AFTERNOON WHEN I WAS 13 YEARS OLD, I ATTRACTED the attention of some bullies as I rode the bus home from school. The older guys sneakily tied the cords of my coat to the seat so that when I tried to stand to get up, I found myself stuck and missed my stop. I was raging, and it seemed as if everyone was laughing at me; just what I needed on top of the vulnerability I already felt, being new to the area. However, what was then a humiliating experience soon opened the door to a new world of possibility. From that day on, with a cautious blessing from my parents, hitching became my primary mode of school transport until my family eventually moved closer to town.

But hitching was not only a means of avoiding confrontation with school bullies, and it wasn't just for fun or adventure; it was mainly a practical way of getting from one place to another. Back then, fewer people owned cars, and public transport was scarce. Hitchhiking was a natural alternative in those quieter, slower times when people weren't so wary of lending a hand. You might end up waiting a long time in the rain, but eventually, you'd reach your destination.

Community spirit was a prominent feature of life in decades past, in part out of necessity: people either stuck together or perished alone.

Neighbours often helped each other through the *meitheal*, the old Irish term for work sharing. My grandmother used to tell us stories about the neighbours who helped build her family's house. Offering the same kindness in return, my gran's family would pitch in with farm work, and so the wheel of reciprocity and interdependence kept turning.

Hitchhiking always felt to me like a natural part of this web of interconnectedness. It exemplifies that sense that we're all in it together – that we can pick someone up when they need help, as it might be us or someone we know who needs help tomorrow. I experienced this each Saturday morning during my teens when I would hitch 24 kilometres from Cootehill to Cavan town to play rugby. I'd usually end up walking and waiting for half an hour or more before getting a lift, and the same on the way back, but I thought nothing of it. In an era before smartphones or the internet, it was as if I had all the time in the world. In later years, hitching opened up the world to me when I travelled in Scotland, Canada, Australia, New Zealand and West Africa. I gained insight into other people and cultures, and developed confidence, conversational skills and the capacity for trust.

Times changed, though. As the years passed, hitching slowly disappeared from my life and, seemingly, from the world around me. The more money I earned, the lazier I became, opting for comfort and convenience over the occasional hardships of thumbs-out travel. As the Irish economy blossomed, people bought cars and public transport improved somewhat. Urbanisation, individualism and the pressures of modern life also set in, and with these, hitchhiking faded into the past.

The demise of hitching was aided by movies and news reports that pushed a particular narrative, suggesting hitchhikers might be dangerous people, or that they themselves stood a good chance of being attacked by opportunistic drivers.

I wasn't entirely immune to the fear factor. I understood that safety could be a concern, especially for women. My experiences as a man could not compare – a sobering reminder that all is not equal and just in the world. I had encountered a few creepy drivers over the years, and while I managed to get away from them by trusting my gut and asking to be dropped off early, these kinds of experiences had left me more sceptical, cynical and cautious than desired. Keeping an open heart was important to me. I always loved the line from the Edgar Guest poem, 'Faith', that reads, 'Strangers are friends that we some day may meet'. I had seen, though, how easy it was to become closed off in order to protect myself.

When I first told people of my plans to hitch around Ireland, common responses included 'Aren't you afraid of being murdered?' and 'Nobody hitches anymore.' Whether hitchhiking was dead or not was a valid question, and one that I was keen to investigate. I didn't doubt that dangers existed, but I also wasn't fully convinced that people were now too busy, mistrustful or selfish to bother giving lifts. I liked the idea of challenging conventional wisdom – of putting my thumb out to the nation to see what it stood for. In doing so, I would be reconnecting with my youthful openness, healing old wounds, and inviting my country to reveal itself.

———

It was the end of June, but the weather was more fitting for January. When I arrived at my mother's house, rain pounded down relentlessly from the dark Connemara skies. With weather like this, I thought, I'd be better off hitching in sunny Spain, or else abandoning the adventure altogether. But I had momentum now; things were moving forward and there was no turning back.

The perfect launch point for my trip had fallen into my lap when I was invited to speak at a community event in County Galway, and it came just in time. The MacGill conference was only a month away, so I'd need to hit the road soon if I was to make it around Ireland before then. My mother Ann lived in Spiddal, near Galway City, and I figured I'd spend a few days there catching up with her before venturing further west. Beyond that, I had no idea what direction I'd take, literally or figuratively. This thought conjured the right mix of nerves and excitement to suggest I'd made the right decision.

'Look who it is! The wild rover,' my mother joked when I arrived at her house. 'This trip of yours sounds very exciting. I'm dying to hear all about it.' She had supported my adventures unflinchingly over the years, and it felt good to spend some time with her before hitting the road. She had also been a huge source of inspiration to me, particularly in recent years, and her story was very much about hope.

My mother used to manage an advice service for people experiencing financial difficulties, but after separating from my father several years back, she knew it was time for a change. Seeking to improve her health, she discovered kinesiology, Qi Gong and meditation and found herself studying the world of health and healing. Though her healing gifts felt new to her, they came as no surprise to those who knew her. The truth was, she had been healing people for years, employing her calming presence to help her clients who struggled with debt.

During this same period, my mother would often visit my younger sister, Sinéad, who was at college in Galway. During one of these visits, she decided to venture further west of Galway City and out to the Irish-speaking village of Spiddal (An Spidéal) where she spent the night at a bed and breakfast. Little did she know, this unplanned visit to Spiddal was to begin a life-changing detour.

'You'd better be careful, Ann,' the owner of the bed and breakfast warned her on her first morning there. 'Some people come here and don't go back. It happened to an artist from Galicia in Spain called Jesús who first stayed here with me, too. He ended up staying for years and was the driving force behind the Spiddal Craft Village in Spiddal.'

'Don't tempt me,' my mother replied. She had grown up by the sea in Bundoran, County Donegal, and had always dreamed of returning to the coast, having moved inland to Cavan when she was only 18 years old. With the story of Jesús Modia, a seed had been planted.

Yet it all seemed like an impossible dream. The housing market had collapsed, and my mother still had a large mortgage to pay off, with no significant savings or pension pot to tap into. Besides, she was in her mid-fifties and knew nobody in these parts.

Sometime later, home in County Cavan, she was on her way to work one morning when a van appeared out of nowhere and nearly killed her. The accident served as a major, albeit severe, wake-up call, causing her to reflect on where she was going in life and what she really wanted.

It was during this time that she viewed a rental house in Spiddal 'just for fun', and within days she had quit her job and started packing her bags.

'It all just happened,' she told me later. 'It was as if I was being guided by angels. It's hard to believe now when I look back on it all.' Four years on, here she was in Spiddal, running the Ionad Bhríde healing centre overlooking Galway Bay and living a life she had once considered impossible. Her journey hadn't always been easy, but it served as a constant example that it's never too late to take a chance and seek happiness.

The day after I arrived in Spiddal, I headed into Galway City to meet a guy named Ross. At the suggestion of a journalist friend, I had decided to record my conversations with people I met along the way. Lacking a recording device, I posted on social media asking if anyone had an audio recorder they could lend me. Within seconds my post was being shared all over the place by people eager to help – contemporary community spirit in action.

Eventually, a woman called Muireann sourced a recording device and Ross jumped in to say he'd collect it and deliver it to me. Meeting him in Galway, I was immediately struck by his youth. He was only 16 years old, but our initial exchange made it clear that Ross was a wise soul. 'I'm on my way to the Crann Og Eco Farm near Gort,' he told me. 'I'm into eco-building and architecture and I'm volunteering there, as they don't teach you that stuff at school.'

I was impressed by and a little jealous of his calmness and confidence. *If only I had had that kind of clarity and drive at 16*, I thought. Here was a guy who truly embodied that old adage, 'Where your talents and the needs of the world cross, there lies your purpose.'

While I hadn't yet begun hitchhiking, Ross seemed a natural first candidate to hear from. I asked his permission to turn on the newly acquired recorder and questioned him about his views on Ireland and his source of hope for the future.

'My view on things,' he told me, 'is mostly focused on the education system. I want Ireland to be more eco-friendly, especially when it comes to building. The school system doesn't teach this, and it should. I just feel like people are living ten years in the past, not looking to the future. That's what I want to look at when I leave school – to give people a different way of living.'

Ross drew his inspiration from a family-friendly festival called Earth Song, where teens are given their own space to camp and then join their families or guardians for meals and events. 'After the last Earth Song festival, a group of us teens got together and went to a hostel in Wicklow to have our own gathering. We ended up with 32 of us and a few parental guardians. We had different kinds of workshops, like drumming, with communal meals and talking-stick circles where everyone gets to share how they're feeling. We did another one down in Leitrim, and it went great. It's especially good that the younger and older people get to join together.'

I could see now how the Earth Song festival, which I had previously regarded as being overly hippie-ish, represented an important intergenerational alternative in a culture that often neglects its responsibility to youth. Instead of treating younger people as mere nuisances or consumers, Earth Song provided them with a sense of ownership, empowerment and inclusion.

Meeting Ross was perfect serendipity: a bright young person with a clear vision for Ireland was kick-starting my listening tour and sending me off with an infectious sense of hope. As it turned out, I wasn't the only one inspired by our conversation. When I uploaded the interview online a few days later, it was quickly shared. A national radio station played a clip, followed by a TV station, bringing Ross's inspirational message to hundreds of thousands of people. The ripple effect was impressive. A teenager replies to a social media post, delivers a recording device to a stranger, and the next thing you know, he's influencing the nation.

Seeing the potential in what was unfolding, I started to feel more alive than I had in ages. A fog was lifting, and I felt excitement in my bones. There was something special about this trip that was already snapping me out of my rut, satisfying a part of me that craved more adventure, spontaneity, and community connection.

———

Bolstered by the success of my first interview, I walked the narrow, winding streets of Galway looking for more opportunities while trying to figure out how I might best approach people. The streets were alive: the combination of fun-loving locals, musicians and tourists always contributed to an electric yet relaxed atmosphere that was unlike anywhere else in Ireland.

On Shop Street I stopped a couple of young women handing out flyers. They were from Belfast, they explained, born-again Christians, in Galway to 'spread the good news'. Maintaining hope wasn't an issue for them, they said: 'Jesus is all we need.'

Across the street from the public park area of Eyre Square, I edged towards a market stall trader selling wallets, hats, jewellery and mobile phone holders. He appeared to be in his sixties, with a face full of stories and a twinkle in his eye.

'There are a lot of people out there who, if they won the lotto in the morning, would still complain that they didn't get enough,' he told me with a big, cheeky smile. 'If people would go the other way, and use their initiative and be more positive about life, they would be much happier.' I had to hand it to him. There was plenty to moan about, but this man's cheerful demeanour spoke volumes about the value of attitude in shaping our reality.

Later, I came across a group of protesters on their way to the Garda (Irish police) station. 'We're going to lodge a complaint against the corrupt bankers for defrauding the country,' one of them said, handing me a template letter outlining their demands. It requested criminal charges be brought against the heads of the Anglo Irish Bank, specifically for 'defrauding the Irish people of €7 billion'.

This issue had dominated the news for days, and though the public was enraged, little was being done. 'What else do we need to know?' asked a determined-looking, grey-haired woman. 'We shouldn't just sit there and take this. The law is the law, and it needs to be upheld. The authorities have a duty to investigate and to prosecute, as they have done in the US and Iceland.'

'Do you want to come with us?' she asked.

I hesitated. I hadn't envisaged starting my trip by getting involved in some kind of legal case against bankers. While I agreed with the protesters, I knew the letter was unlikely to be taken seriously. In my heart, I shared some of the resignation and fatigue felt by so many. Too often, people with power, status and influence had abused their positions in society without consequence. But what was I to do? Give up hope? Accept the situation, maintain a positive attitude and ignore injustice? Or carry out a civic ritual by signing the letter and being part of the calls for change? Maybe it would have no impact – but then again, maybe it would be the beginning of a ripple that could become a wave. So in I went to the Galway Garda station, where I signed the letter and handed it to a bemused-looking Garda on desk duty. Perhaps it was only symbolic, but at least I was contributing a small push to turning the wheels of justice.

It had been a jam-packed day in Galway, and I was feeling energised and excited for the next stage. I was also hungry, and my mother had a big meal waiting for me back in Spiddal. I appreciated the opportunity to fatten up for the road ahead, but had to admit I was starting to feel like a bit of a Mammy's boy. I knew I'd have to get out there soon and stick that thumb to the wind.

————

After dinner that evening, I parked my mother's car near the beach in Spiddal as the clouds lifted over the shimmering dark blue waters of Galway Bay.

As I set off on a walk, I noticed two older men trying to get their car started. I asked if they needed a push, and they replied in Irish with a phrase I didn't understand. The Irish language was never my strong point, but it seemed their English was just as bad.

'*Tá brón orm, níl móran Gaeilge agam,*' I stuttered back as best I could. 'I'm sorry, my Irish is poor.'

They replied again in Irish, but I was lost, humbled my inability to communicate with these fellow Irishmen. We were only a few kilometres from Galway City, and it was extremely rare to encounter non-English speakers – but this was a Gaeltacht, an area where Irish was still the first language, at least for now. A sense of shame and embarrassment crept over me; I felt like a stranger in my own land.

The men seemed relaxed, as though they were used to this kind of situation. No doubt, like many native Irish speakers, they had daily interactions with State agencies and others whom they couldn't readily understand. Several native speakers I know had told me that the difficulty of communicating with government services in Irish was contributing to the decline of the language. I knew this was about more than a loss of words and sounds – it was about the way different cultures perceive and experience the world. Even small, everyday phrases like 'hello' – *Dia dhuit* in Irish – tell us something about the difference in depth of the Irish language. *Dia dhuit*, or 'God be with you', is a greeting imbued with a sense of reverence and blessing that goes beyond religion.

I eventually managed to communicate with the men through eye contact and hand gestures. We all smiled, and I joined one of them to give the car a push start. 'Slán!' I shouted out as they sped off, leaving me deep in thought. I have an Irish name: *Ruairí* – from *rua*, meaning 'red', and *rí*, meaning 'king' – and my encounter with the men had reminded me that I was missing a deeper connection to the language of my ancestors and to different ways of seeing and being.

I hadn't expected my brief stay in Spiddal to awaken such powerful reflections, but it felt fitting. I was about to embark on a journey not only with an eye to Ireland's future, but also to reconnect with my nation's history and tradition.

2

Hitting the Road

Moycullen to Inishbofin

'I'M GOING TO YOGA WITH SUNNY THIS EVENING. YOU should come,' my mother said when I finally returned to her house. I wasn't enthusiastic. My head was in a bit of a spin and I needed to slow down, get organised and prepare for the trip ahead. However, I knew yoga could help ground me a bit. Besides, if this trip was about hope, it would be perfect to meet up again with the teacher, Sunny Jacobs.

I had first come across Sunny in a newspaper article years earlier. Her beaming smile shone out at me from the page, as did the touching message of love and forgiveness that accompanied her roller-coaster story of tragedy and triumph. Originally from the US and now in her late sixties, Sunny had served 17 years in prison for a crime she didn't commit. During this time her husband was executed in the electric chair, her children were taken into foster care, her parents died in a plane crash and she spent five years in solitary confinement.

Yet, despite these horrific experiences, here she was making space for people to experience yoga and meditation – the practices she says offered her a chance to find true freedom in the face of her incarceration.

'It's a great thing that you're doing, Ruairí,' she said to me as I left her class that evening. 'You know, so many people have faced huge hardships in different ways. Often one of the best things you can do for them is to listen to them, to bear witness to their story. Being listened to, and believed, that's something that can help people find hope.'

I was struck by Sunny's message, and resolved that if nothing else, I would seek to bear witness to whoever I might meet on the road ahead.

———

Wind and rain battered the windows of the house the next morning, taunting me as I pondered what the day ahead might bring. My mother, in no rush to get rid of me, had encouraged a stay of another night or two, and my impulse was to roll over and spend the day in bed. *Oh no, you don't!* shouted an internal voice. *Today is the day. Get your ass out of here.*

This was it: time to get moving.

Pulling on a new bright yellow raincoat for the first time, I laughed at the sight of myself. I had bought it as an experiment, hoping the yellow would make me more visible to traffic. I looked more like a German tourist, which I reasoned would make pick-ups more likely.

I wasn't exactly heading for Antartica, but my mother seemed a little sad as she drove me to Moycullen, from where I would set off on the road west. 'It's been so good having you here for a couple of days, Ruairí. May the road ahead be blessed for you. I hope your your quest is nothing but magical,' she said. As we waved goodbye, it hit me that the trip was finally beginning.

———

The moment I put my thumb out to the wind, a sense of freedom descended. The drizzle falling on my face brought back memories of the countless hours I had stood on the side of the road waiting for lifts. I had passed the time when younger making up games to predict what kind of car would come next, creating new ways to stand or to hold my thumb, imagining how I could influence the odds of getting picked up.

Hitching may be the activity that has taught me the most about how to interact with diverse people and discover shared interests. I remember lifts from farmers, travelling salespeople, tourists, and families on their way to football matches. I never knew who was going to pick me up, or what the topic of conversation would be. Once, when I was about 15 years old, I got a lift from an Irish guy on leave from the French Foreign Legion. Unaware, at the time, of the controversial history of this particular military force, I remember being in awe of the man's adventurous life and the fact that a person like me, from rural Ireland, could end up travelling the world and living in an entirely different way.

Here I was, decades later, back at the side of the road with my thumb in the air. I was starting to daydream about the trip when suddenly I noticed a van had pulled in on the roadside just metres ahead to give me a lift.

I rushed towards the van and looked in the passenger side window as the driver edged towards me. 'How's it goin'? Where are you headed?' said the friendly-looking man in a strong Galway accent.

'I'm heading out west – actually, I'm not too sure yet,' I replied, realising it might be better to have a destination in mind.

'I'm going as far as Oughterard, so it'll get you on your way. Hop in.'

I hadn't figured out a route or taken time to think about where I was going. This was mostly a conscious choice. I wanted to go with the flow and allow each day to determine what places I'd visit, whom I would meet and where I would sleep. I was at the mercy of the universe. I trusted I would end up talking to whoever I needed to talk to, hearing whatever stories needed to be heard.

'So, are you on holidays, or what are you up to?' the driver asked.

'I'm, eh . . .' I stumbled. 'I'm doing a bit of a trip around Ireland,' I said, noting again that I would need a clearer answer to what was sure to become an all-too-common question. 'I actually only started about a few minutes ago, and you're my first lift,' I said, as the driver looked at me with intrigue.

'Jasus, that sounds interesting. G'wan, tell me more,' he said with genuine curiosity.

'Well, I'm involved in all sorts of youth and community work, and I was asked to give a talk up in Donegal. I decided I'd go around

Ireland as part of my research for the talk. It's fairly unplanned but I'm generally looking at the topic of hope – I want to know if people are hopeful for the future of Ireland, and if so, where they find hope. If that makes any sense. . .'

I paused. I wasn't sure how my spiel would land. Was I coming across as some sort of weirdo or lost wanderer, or was my first go at explaining myself clear enough? Then again, the interviews in Galway had gone well, and most people I'd met seemed very open to talking. 'Fair play to ya,' the man replied, instantly easing my fears. 'That sounds like a great project. I wouldn't mind doing something like that myself.' Not only was David, my driver, enthused about my mission, he was also keen to share his views on the state of the nation.

'Looking back at the last few years and the promises that were made, nothing seems to have changed at the top,' he explained as we made our way along the twists and turns of the N59. 'The same people that caused the problems are still at the top. I suppose it's like any problem: unless you get to the source of it, you're not going to stop it. They're still there. They're just moving them around with window dressing and telling us things will be fine. I don't think things will be, not when the same people are in charge.'

I understood David's frustration. A builder by trade, work had slowed down but he had found an intriguing way of bringing in extra income: 'I'm doing a bit of beekeeping now to supplement myself,' he revealed, to my surprise. 'My father was a beekeeper, so it's in the blood. It's good for the head, kind of spiritual. We can learn a lot from bees and how well organised they are. There's no real money in it, but with a good summer like this, it can be alright. On a day like this, they'll be working the blackberry, and the meadowsweet wildflower.'

He went quiet for a moment, as if lost in thought imagining the bees on their way from flower to flower.

'There's always someone worse off than you. I'm not too badly off,' he continued. 'Still, when you work hard all your life and get hammered left, right and centre, and then see all these fat cats at the top . . . that's the way the world is,' he said, growing more serious and impassioned.

'I've never had allegiance to any particular political party. It's all about greed and power. When you see what the multinationals are doing, and the bankers – they're controlling the lot and not telling us the truth. I'd like the Taoiseach to stick to what he said he'd do. No cronyism for once, and to stand up to the bankers. I wouldn't be voting for them again, nor Labour.'

As we pulled up in Oughterard, David's thoughts returned to the bees, and he offered a parting message as passionate as anything I'd heard in a while. 'Bees are so important for the planet and for food systems,' he began. 'A huge amount of the food on the planet is pollinated by bees and other insects. If they become extinct, as is happening in America and China, then we'll have a major problem. People don't realise this. They just think bees will sting them, and they try to hit them with newspapers,' he stated matter-of-factly.

'We're lucky in Ireland that we don't have too many modified crops being grown here, but companies like Monsanto are treating the seeds with insecticide before they are even sown,' he continued. 'That insecticide is carried up into the flower, and the bee then takes the nectar, so that in effect it's contaminated by the insecticide. The bee then carries the contamination back to the line – and they wonder why bee colonies are collapsing around the world. You don't need a scientist to figure it out,' David pronounced with indignation.

'But Monsanto, one of the most powerful companies on the planet, doesn't want to hear that. They have the government in America, and probably here as well, in their back pockets. The government was testing genetically modified potatoes down in Carlow, but we don't need GM. Haven't we grown crops here since the Ice Age? People talk about the famine, but we've got that sorted – that was blight, and that's under control. The aim now is to control all the seeds on the planet. The way I see it is Big Pharma sprays our food with chemicals, and then when we get sick, they sell us drugs and chemicals to keep us alive – it's a win-win for them.' David was on a roll, as if he'd been studying all this for years and was hungry to share what he had discovered.

'But genetically modified crops aren't solving world hunger. If they were concerned about world hunger, they wouldn't be acting the way they are now. They just wouldn't. They want to control farmers by making them buy all these modified seeds. But they don't go to seed, so you have to buy seeds every year from Monsanto or whoever is making them. So they really have you. It's about control. There's a few at the top, and they want to control everything. If you look here at the Church and the whole lot, they all want control.'

While there was no doubting the power imbalance David discussed, neither was there any doubt that people like him could help shift it. By educating himself, investing in beekeeping, and sharing the knowledge he cultivated, he was contributing in a significant way. I had barely begun my trip and already I had found a social pollinator of sorts, a man spreading seeds of hope and helping to create fertile conditions for change.

———

The streets of Oughterard, a small market town, were busy with tourists, tractors and locals carrying out their day-to-day business. It was nearly lunchtime, and my stomach was starting to talk.

I had just finished paying for a sandwich inside a local shop when I heard a voice call out, 'Hey Ruairí, good to see you!' I turned around and saw a young, black-haired man smiling at me. 'My name is Jonathan. I was at one of your talks a while back. Small world, eh?' he said. 'I loved all that stuff you were talking about around community power and all of that. That's a big theme for our town right now.' Jonathan invited me across the road to the local one-room tourism office where he was volunteering.

There, I ate my sandwich and listened as he spoke excitedly about the tourism training course he had recently completed. He explained that the government-funded tourism office had closed due to lack of funding. Volunteers had come together to create this new service in Oughterard, an important gateway town for the popular Connemara region. 'We just opened two weeks ago. I did a seven-month course here at the local Youthreach centre and got offered this job as part of the course. I'm only here three days so far and I love it.' It was great to witness Jonathan's energy and enthusiasm and to see how a volunteer-run initiative was bringing life back to this rural town.

Jonathan introduced me to a friend who had been hovering beside a shelf full of tourist brochures in the simple yet welcoming office. Brandy was in her early twenties and spoke with a blended accent: part Galwegian, part American. 'I moved here as a minor at 10 years of age about 12 years ago and never knew anything about immigration. My mother is American, and my stepfather is Irish – but the problem is that my stepfather never adopted me. I thought I was okay, that I was under my mother's stamp or something. I didn't realise I needed a stamp after the age of 16.

'When I reached 18 and started applying for college and everything, my mother realised that I was illegally here. I decided to go to Immigration and try to get things sorted out by applying to become a naturalised citizen. I've been waiting nearly three years now. It's been very hard to be told I'm an illegal immigrant even though my naturalisation has been accepted, and after paying for it with a loan of €950,' Brandy lamented.

'The fear you go through every day as an undocumented immigrant is amazing. I can't go to college and I can't work. I can't claim anything from the State, and I'm living here on my own now. I have an apartment to keep up, and I have to do something. That means I have to break the law in order to survive. The fear of that is unbelievable. I mean, what happens if I get caught? Am I going to be deported? Do I not have a right to live? Do I not have a right to eat? I don't think it's very fair.' Brandy paused in reflection.

'I love Ireland – it's my home. It has been for 12 years, and it will be for many years to come,' she said, her Galway accent underlining her determination to remain. 'It's a beautiful place with lovely people, but something needs to be sorted with the immigration part.'

I asked Brandy what the future might look like for her. 'It's a shame that young people are emigrating, but there are no jobs,' she replied. 'I'd like to finish college and not have to deal with €10,000 non-EU student fees I was being asked for. I'd be interested in studying psychology. As a child I got counselling, and I really like what counsellors do. It really opened my mind. I like helping people.'

I had encountered similar stories: young people who had fallen between the cracks of an immigration system that is desperately under-resourced and inefficient. The situation is far worse for asylum seekers – people who often spend years in the soul-crushing system known as direct provision. In this system, residents are given a small weekly living allowance but aren't allowed to work. They share cramped rooms in generally run-down buildings that lack adequate facilities, services and supports – a kind of institutionalised limbo land where people are powerless to improve their circumstances.

'We are dying slowly in here,' an asylum seeker from DR Congo told me outside a direct provision centre in Donegal several years ago. He explained how many of his fellow residents had escaped war, conflict and persecution, only to end up in overcrowded facilities with no money and a constant fear of deportation. 'The system crushes your spirit. Yes, we have food and a bed, but we cannot live as normal humans. People lose their minds. It is no surprise that there have been many suicides in this system.'

Brandy's circumstances were clearly different from this man's. She was white, with an American/Galwegian accent; she could blend into a crowd with relative ease; and she wasn't locked inside an oppressive facility. Yet her mind was occupied by worries that didn't fit her profile. 'I'm afraid the Garda are going to knock on my door some night,' she said with an anxious shake in her voice. 'I'm stressed, and it's really getting to me.' By all appearances, a carefree young person, Brandy's inner world was a whirlwind of worry. Speaking with her, I was reminded of the aphorism, 'Be kind, for everyone you meet is fighting a battle you know nothing about.'

———

After saying goodbye to Jonathan and Brandy, I started to make my way out of town but was distracted by a sign pointing to the local youth centre. I figured it was worth dropping by. At this rate, I wasn't going to get far today, but I was loving the freedom to follow my nose and go with the flow.

Inside the large, colourful building, a youth worker named Barry told me about the important role the centre plays in providing a safe and welcoming space for young people to meet and get involved in activities that help them realise their potential. Interested in his perspective, I asked him my big question. 'Where's the hope coming from?' 'Phew! That's a big question to come in the door with,' he responded with a smile. 'Well, we work with young people up to 25, through arts, sport, and education. We have a youth café and this week we have a youth arts festival. We've identified the arts as a really effective way of working with young people, through film, music, poetry and visual art. We also do CoderDojo computer programming.'

Barry also talked about one of the biggest problems he encounters in his work. 'Alcohol is such a huge issue. Young people are being more exposed to it. There's a culture around it; it's like a rite of passage, a social norm, even for the mid-teens. We try to counter that by providing alcohol-free activities. Some young people have told us that they often fall in with the crowd drinking because the alternatives just aren't there, so our focus is on creating them. To do that we need volunteers, community buy-in – everyone needs to get behind it. It's not just young people; it's a cultural thing and a generational thing. It's so easy to say young people are this or that, but behaviour filters down. I think we can change the attitudes of young people if we change the attitudes of the older people.'

Listening to Barry, I was reminded of my own work. Time after time I had seen the need for intergenerational connection – young people who needed guidance from elders, and elders who could benefit from the ideas and energy of our youth.

'I love this work. It doesn't feel like a job,' Barry said as our conversation came to an end. I admired his commitment. I knew that people in this field were rarely well paid, yet it is people like Barry who help weave the fabric of communities together.

I had barely resumed my departure from Oughterard when a pair of women wearing fluorescent work vests greeted me with big smiles.

They were busy painting a fine old townhouse building that had fallen into disrepair.

'We're part of the Tidy Towns group,' one of the women said to me with a mix of humility and pride. 'We're just trying to improve the derelict buildings here in the town. This building is owned by a family that no longer lives here – some are dead, some have moved away. We want to put a nice face on these places, to bring them back to what they were. It's all voluntary. We have a great interest in how the place should look. We have to get back to volunteering, the way it was many years ago.'

There was clearly no shortage of problems on people's minds, but there was evidently an abundance of people willing to stand up and work together, either. Time would tell if perhaps Oughterard was unique in this regard. I hoped not.

———

As I arrived on the outskirts of town, rain started to fall and the road was eerily quiet. The few cars that did pass just sped on by, not taken by me or my bright yellow jacket. *Ah, now I remember*, I thought, as memories of so many cold moments on the roadside came back. Yes, hitching evoked nostalgia, but also misery – recollections of standing in the wind, rain and cold, wondering why so many people drove past as if they hadn't seen you.

In my teenage days, I'd avert boredom during these stretches by talking to myself, singing, and making up games. I'd think up all sorts of stories and scenarios, imagining where the people who passed me by might be going. Perhaps the man in the blue car was on his way to hospital, as his wife had just had a baby. Or maybe the couple in the silver Toyota was having an affair and couldn't stop because things would be too awkward. Possibly the first thing on some people's minds was whatever negative news story they had heard about hitchhiking, or maybe they just needed some quiet head space. I could certainly identify with the latter.

In the rare times I had to wait more than an hour, I'd often start walking, thinking it better to make some progress than stand staring at the road. In those moments alone, ideas would emerge: new visions of things I wanted to accomplish, or thoughts of a girl at school who had caught my attention. But the other side of my mind also showed itself – the one where doubts, fears, and self-criticism dwelt, making me want to avoid solitude. Had I known about mindfulness at the age of 14 or 15, perhaps I could have navigated the kaleidoscope of teenage thoughts in my mind each day with greater wisdom.

Standing in the rain on this bleak July day, as passing cars splashed puddles onto my jeans, I smiled as I realised how much hitching can teach us about life: most importantly, the ability to be comfortable in our own minds when we realise that much of the journey is outside our control.

———

Eventually, a flashy, black four-wheel-drive pulled over. In my experience, it was less common for people in fancier cars to stop for hitchhikers, but there were, of course, exceptions. John, from the south side of Dublin, was one of those.

He was on his way to meet some friends for a weekend of kayaking. 'I'm going to Cleggan if that's any use to you?' he asked through the window.

'That'll do,' I replied as I jumped in, recalling that the main feature in Cleggan was perhaps the ferry port to Inishbofin island. *Fantastic!* I thought. *A trip to Inishbofin, that would be amazing!*

I liked the thought of being transported from one island, Ireland, to this very small one for my first proper night on the road. I had heard great things about Inishbofin, and even the name felt warm and endearing. Like most Irish place names, it was an anglicisation of the Irish language – in this case, Inis Bó Finne, or 'island of the white cow.' However, I kind of liked the idea of Inishbofin as an island of *boffins*: mad scientists and geeks with their own sort of Harry Potter–style alternative reality.

'Yes, you can't go wrong with Inishbofin, I'd highly recommend it,' John said to me when I told him my idea. John was a lawyer in his mid-thirties, about my age, and had previously been involved in the tourism business. 'I used to hitch loads myself. I hitched most of the way to Istanbul once,' he said, as if it was no big deal. 'From Ireland?!' I replied. 'Yeah, I got the ferry to France and hitched on from there with the odd bus and train here and there,' he said, before regaling me with the tale of a lift from a horse and cart owner among other adventures.

Wow, I thought. *Now that's a real hitching adventure.* That horrible feeling of inadequacy threatened to overcome me, but fortunately, I caught it in time, reminding myself that living through comparison is nonsense.

We travelled on over the bumpy Connemara roads, past the tiny village of Recess, looking out over Derryclare Lake and the Twelve Bens mountain range to our right. 'You're right to get out there talking to people,' John said. 'So many politicians are out of touch. I considered running in the last election,' he confessed. 'I had been involved in some community campaigns and figured it's important that people like us run for election. However, in the end, I decided it wasn't for me. But I think it's so important to find ways of engaging people with what's happening in this country.'

Before we continued on to nearby Cleggan, John made a quick stop in Clifden to pick up supplies. Inside the local supermarket, I was filling my basket when I spotted some young tourists warming their hands under a heat lamp that was also warming roasted chickens. I laughed out loud and they made eye contact, their misery turning to laughter over the silliness of the situation. 'Ah, welcome to Ireland,' I said, smiling. 'I see you've encountered our fine summer weather.'

———

An eerie evening mist descended upon the seaside village of Cleggan as John dropped me off. I walked down the main street, bought a ticket and made my way back to board the small ferry, immediately filled with a child-like excitement at the prospect of sailing out to sea. It took me back to the times I had taken the boat from Dublin to Wales during my teens, or from Belfast to Scotland when I was at university there, in the era before cheap airfares and busier lives. There was something ancient and primal about travelling on water. I thought about the Vikings, various invaders to our shores, emigrants and explorers, and the fishermen once so plentiful in these parts, imagining a time when waterways were the highways for trade and travel.

The wind hit my face as we set off – about 20 locals and tourists – across the choppy waves. It felt good to be back at sea. After about 20 minutes sailing under wild and mysterious dark blue skies, a cluster of imposing stone ruins set among rocky slopes came into view: Inishbofin peeked out from beyond the mist. It felt like we were travelling into another time, to a curious place with all sorts of stories to tell.

Arriving at the Inishbofin pier, I felt giddy. I had had no idea, waking up in Spiddal earlier that morning, that I'd end the day on this intriguing little island.

The darkening sky interrupted my reverie, and I set out to find somewhere to stay. I followed a sign to the backpackers' hostel and walked up a narrow, winding roadway that climbed between stone walls and small rocky fields.

Ten minutes later, in the shelter of the hostel, the friendly young woman in charge offered me a cup of tea and a freshly baked muffin before showing me to my room. 'You can take the top bunk to your right or the bottom one at the back,' she said. 'Thanks very much,' I replied, though the comfort afforded by the tea and muffin began to fade. I gazed in despair at the cramped room and fought off the smell of socks, sweat and other odours I preferred not to identify.

I had stayed in dozens of these places over the years, but the older I got, the more I found myself abandoning hostels in favour of bed and breakfasts or hotels. Hostels, to me, belonged to the world of 21-year-olds travelling the world with their Lonely Planet guides and a thirst for booze, sex and adventure. There were those who figured they could get away with a little romantic rumble in their bunk without anyone noticing, and those who fell in drunk at 3am. Then, at 6am, the noisy go-getters would start packing for a day's hiking. I had been there, done that, and while it had been fun, it was not the type of adventure I was after this time.

I took a peek outside and calculated the odds of being able to pitch my tent without getting soaked. I decided to go for it and set up in the back garden to enjoy its relative privacy and quiet. After lots of clumsy fumbling, I finally made sense of the 'one-person' tent I had purchased in Galway. I squeezed my rucksack inside and wormed my way in, laughing. The tent was smaller than anything I'd ever used – more like a canvas coffin. With my rucksack squashed into the spot where my legs needed to go, I lay back, snuggled into my sleeping bag and reflected on a great first day on the road.

3

Finding Damo

Inishbofin

A FURIOUS HOWLING AND BANGING SHOOK ME FROM my sleep. *What the hell is going on?* I thought, panicking momentarily as I struggled to remember where I was. It didn't take long for the fierce Atlantic wind and rain to remind me that I was inside a tiny tent. I had fallen asleep, only to be awoken before dawn by this ferocious storm. I lay there shivering, hoping that I might somehow get back to sleep.

At 5.30am, after an optimistic half hour, I gave up. *How quickly the romance fades*, I noted as I made my way towards the hostel's main door, which I could only hope had been left open. The previous day had flowed so smoothly. Now here I was, starting the day cold, wet, and tired, feeling foolish for having turned down a warm bed. Thankfully the front door was open, and I decided I'd make myself a hot drink in the kitchen to warm up. That bright idea was soon torpedoed by a locked door and a sign that read, 'The kitchen opens at 8am daily.'

I stood there licking my wounds, trying to imagine how I might get through that locked door to the hot coffee I imagined lay beyond. Just as I had run out of ideas and started to plan my escape from the island on the first ferry, a hallway door opened and out bounced a cheery, bearded man. 'Good morning to ya!' he exclaimed. 'How are ya? Did you arrive last night?' The man, named Brendan, looked to be in his fifties but had the energy of a spring lamb despite having slept in a tent out back just as I had tried to do. I hadn't noticed him at the opposite end of the campsite.

'Would you like a coffee?' he asked, revealing that he had the keys to the kitchen. Suddenly, the day had taken a new twist. 'What about some porridge? Let me get you some porridge. I have a special recipe that you have to taste. It's got a mix of the best Irish oats with stewed cinnamon, fennel seeds, bananas, blackberries – you won't find better!' he exclaimed as my stomach sang with happiness. As we entered the kitchen, I told Brendan about my experience of being pummelled by the previous night's storm, which he seemed to have survived unscathed. As it turned out, he had the help of a luxurious inflatable mattress and two sleeping bags, one a metre wide at the foot. 'You're not set up right at all, Ruairí. You need the right gear. I sleep really well each night. Besides, I'm always exhausted after my daily activities,' he said.

Within minutes, my self-pity had evaporated and I was sipping hot coffee and eating what seemed like Ireland's best porridge as Brendan gave me the lowdown. 'I love it here,' he told me, explaining that he was staying on Inishbofin for the summer and helping out in the hostel. 'I go for a run in the mornings. Then I go out on the kayak and do a bit of fishing, and then some cooking in the evening. It's a great life,' he said, his eyes sparkling. 'I was made redundant from work in November. So now I have time. I'd been coming to the island for years, and this was the first opportunity to come for a season – so I'm grabbing it with open arms.' It was refreshing to meet someone with such a zest for life, and I warmed to Brendan quickly as he continued to share his story. 'I'm a fishing enthusiast and a forager, and all this activity has left me immensely fulfilled. There's an abundance of life in and around the island, like cockles, winkles and shrimp. Basically, every day, all I'm concerned about is the next meal.

'I was 17 years at the one company. They were looking for voluntary redundancies, but nobody volunteered. I knew I was vulnerable. I was at an awkward age and I was replaceable. I had a feeling the company was going to pick me, and they did. The most important thing is I still have my health,' Brendan concluded with a sense of heartfelt gratitude.

Eventually, I got around to the question of hope. While Brendan wasn't keen to discuss the state of the nation (a topic he said bored the hell out of him), as he spoke, he revealed himself as a deep thinker with a big heart. 'I don't envy people who are struggling,' he said. 'I come from an estate close to Moyross in Limerick. I saw a lot of underprivileged kids who will never get the opportunities I'm enjoying, which isn't a lot – just basic outdoor pursuits. That's very sad.

'I took five city kids out fishing last year and got them involved in gutting the fish. I got them to cook the fish, present it on saucers and offer the fish to their parents. They've been eating fish since. It was a massive experience for them. It was a massive experience for me, too, to be able to contribute at the awkward age they're at. It's a tough age, around 15 years old. They'll remember it, and the old guy who brought them out. For me, hope comes down to simplicity – just simplicity.'

When I told Brendan I'd been thinking of taking the first boat out, he wasn't having any of it. 'Aw now, come on – you've only just arrived! A few of us are cooking up a big dinner of fresh fish tonight, and you should stay and join us. Besides, you haven't even seen any of the island yet.' How could I say no to this man? It was still early morning and already his kindness had transformed my day and had me feeling excited about my trip again. 'Aw sure, why not?' I responded. 'Thanks, Brendan, I really appreciate it. I'll see you this evening.'

———

I set out to explore the island for the day, but as it turned out, my first adventure was waiting right outside the hostel in the form of a small tour group. Approaching one of the members, I asked what the occasion was. 'I'm here for Sea Week; it's amazing,' said the young teacher from Carlow. 'I've been coming here for years.' She explained that Sea Week, along with Bog Week and other cultural festivals held on the island, was the brainchild of a retired Connemara school principal and community activist named Leo Hallissey. He'd been creating festivals for years, attracting hundreds of visitors to the region and boosting employment while simultaneously celebrating Connemara's rich ecology, culture and heritage. 'I'm telling ya, if rural Ireland had more people like Leo, we'd all be better off,' she said enthusiastically.

My curiosity piqued, I asked if I could tag along for a leg of the tour. 'Sure, come on and join us. There's a talk happening down the road.' Off we went down a quiet, meandering roadway, the bright blue Atlantic flickering in the distance. Now that the weather had calmed, I could see how easy it was to fall under Inishbofin's spell.

At the bottom of a field, I joined several teachers amid the roofless ruins of St. Colman's monastery, site of a fourteenth-century abbey and cemetery. Here we met Michael Gibbons, a self-described 'journeyman archaeologist'. I hovered behind the group, a little conscious that I was an imposter among this flock of teachers from all over Ireland. Launching into his talk, Michael explained that Inishbofin had been inhabited for at least 7,000 years and had seen its fair share of drama. The British government, under their notorious penal laws, established a prison for Catholic priests here. The island had also served as a staging post for Irish rebels at various junctures in their quest for independence. Once a more densely populated island, Inishbofin's population had declined from nearly 1,500 people during the famine years of the mid-1800s to fewer than 200 people today.

'Inishark, the neighbouring island, had people on it for 4,000 years,' Michael said, gesturing towards the west. 'It's now abandoned. On Inishturk, a beautiful little island, the school runs a real risk of closing soon due to low student numbers. So the future is kind of bleak unless we really sit down and map out a plan,' said Michael. It was a chilling reminder that traditional ways of life were dying in many parts of Ireland. Everywhere, rural villages were on their knees. The decline of fishing and farming, the emigration of young people, and the closure of pubs, post offices and local shops posed huge challenges. Listening to Michael had hammered home the importance of adopting a historical perspective to understand the country's current state. Just as adults are the products of their childhood experiences, so are nations the products of their history. They are built on the stories, events, loves, losses, wounds and dreams of their past.

I was keen to hear more from Michael, so when the guided tour was over, I asked if I could accompany him on his walk towards the ferry. After I explained the purpose of my journey, Michael said, 'We should consider history in terms of millennia rather than decades. Truly understanding our past is essential if we are to get back on our feet and progress together, not least because of all the storms Ireland has weathered in previous generations. Rebirth is crucial – but this won't be achieved without respecting and learning from those who came before us.' I noted the universality of this message, recalling Charles Seifert's declaration (often attributed to Marcus Garvey) that 'a people without the knowledge of their past history, origin and culture is like a tree without roots'.*

'It's important to know about our culture, to have a real grasp of how the landscape has changed and evolved,' Michael continued. 'We've been living here for 7,000 years, that we know of, with episodic pulses of change that transform the landscape, with society rising, falling, collapsing, and expanding again. We're in one of those periods of transition at the moment. The nineteenth century saw some of our darkest hours, but good things emerged out of it. Out of the ashes of the famine grew the Land League, a political movement to end landlordism and advance tenant rights, and perhaps out of modern-day struggles, new movements might emerge.'

As I stood at the pier, bidding Michael farewell while he boarded the ferry, I noticed a familiar-looking man on the boat: It was Gary, an artist I had met back in May at the annual 'famine walk' commemoration event in Louisburgh, County Mayo. 'I've been here with Damien

---

* Charles Seifert, *The Negro's or Ethiopian's Contribution to Art* (Baltimore, MD: Black Classic Press, 1986), originally published in 1938.

Dempsey and a few of the lads, just swimming, hanging out and playing music for a few days. The lads are still here but I need to head on now,' Gary said.

I was excited to hear that Damien – or Damo, as he is affectionately known – was on the island. I had first come across him ten years earlier when he was performing at a Sinéad O'Connor gig. He held nothing back as he performed 'Celtic Tiger,' a song that lashed out against the greed overtaking the country during the boom years of the mid-1990s. Damo's powerful and passionate performance captivated me, and I became a big fan, admiring his dedication to the folk tradition in the vein of Christy Moore, Pete and Peggy Seeger and Woody Guthrie. He was a voice for the people, and he didn't shy away from songs of protest and struggle in an era when too many artists, record companies, and radio stations preferred safer, more sanitised voices.

Gary told me that Damo was at Murray's pub, five minutes' walk away. I waved goodbye and started in that direction, giddy at the prospect of interviewing the mighty Damo. I appreciated that he was on holiday and I didn't want to be a pain in the ass, but I was hopeful that if I told him what I was up to, he'd agree to at least a short chat.

———

The sun shone brightly as I walked up the road, deep in thought planning my interview. Two female joggers ran past and we greeted each other, as everyone does on the island. Seconds later, one called back, 'Hey, Ruairí, it's me, Róisín, Róisín McGrogan!' I had met Róisín several years ago when she was involved with the Students' Union in Galway, having linked with her on various youth health promotion campaigns. She was on holiday on the island with her mother and sister. She paused for a moment when I asked what she was up to these days. 'I'm taking some time out after quitting my job,' she finally replied. Her hesitancy suggested there was more to the story, but the explanation that followed took me by surprise: 'I'm about to enter the religious life,' she confided. My jaw hit the floor.

'Wow! Are you serious? What do you mean – you're becoming a nun?' I asked, wondering if maybe this was a joke. Hardly anyone chooses to become a nun or a priest these days, especially not people in their twenties, like Róisín.

She was dead serious. 'I have a sense of looking for more, something bigger and more authentic,' she explained. 'I want to be able to be my best self, my true self, and to discover what that is. After college, I volunteered in Calcutta for a while, and while it was a struggle, I took a lot of consolation from prayer, adoration or whatever it is – but I'm not a Holy Joe by any means.' I wondered what it would be like for this intelligent young woman, so accustomed to city life, to give up everything she was used to and completely transform her lifestyle. 'There are three vows: charity, poverty and obedience,' she continued. 'But poverty is sometimes expressed as the freedom to give because you're not attached to material possessions. The way I see it, it's about listening to God – and God as being a spirit within us. So really, it's about being who you truly are. It's so important to take time to stop and listen to who you are, rather than identify yourself with what you do.'

I found it difficult to fully understand Róisín's decision. On the one hand, I could see the appeal in embracing a community and a life that offered more space for solitude and contemplation, away from the busyness of modern life. I knew too the feeling of being called to a vocation, a type of work or a way of living. I felt this myself – a sense of being called to serve others. On the other hand, I was conflicted about what the Church represents. I believed it could be a force for good, but time and again, it seemed to overlook the spirit of love and justice on issues like LGBTQ+ inclusion, contraception, divorce and women's rights. I wondered what Róisín thought about this perspective, but all I could think to say was, 'I wish you well, Róisín.' And I did. She seemed determined to forge her own way, regardless of how unfashionable that path might be. I respected her resolve.

Moments later, I was back on the quest to find Damo. I approached the bright white entrance of Murray's hotel and pub, clearing my throat in preparation for my introduction. But there was no sign of him. I asked at the bar. 'Yeah, you just missed him. He left about five minutes ago. I'm not sure where he's gone.' Evidently, my 'finding Damo' mission, as I had taken to calling it, wasn't going to be simple.

———

Damo had eluded me so far, but Inishbofin was a small island, just 3 kilometres wide and 5.5 kilometres long, and I was sure I could find him. He was a big, tall fella, hopefully easy to spot. Deciding to approach my search mission with a certain nonchalance, I strolled towards the western end of the island to enjoy the afternoon sun. In the near distance, I spotted a man coming down the road who looked like he might be a local. 'Good afternoon, a fine day we're having,' I said as he approached. 'I don't want to bother you, but I'm on a trip around Ireland and wondering if I might ask you a couple of questions on the subject of hope for the country.'

He looked cautious at first, but was soon sharing openly with me, as though happy to have someone who would listen. 'I have two daughters and a son, and the reality is that all of them will probably end up emigrating. That's the reality of life here you know.' You hear about this kind of thing all the time – it's so ingrained in Irish culture, particularly in the west of Ireland – but to think of this man losing close contact with all three children, and possibly future grandchildren, was heart-wrenching.

'It's all pretty simple if you look at it,' he continued in a way that felt familiar. 'The world is run by overlords in economics, politics, and religion. Everyone knows that. The ordinary person doesn't have much say. All you can do is protect your own sanity, and try and keep things simple and free from control. At the end of the day, we don't need much to survive,' he remarked, and I realised he was echoing a sentiment imparted by Brendan earlier that morning. 'That's the way I look at it anyway,' he added, before excusing himself and heading on his way.

Further down the road, I came across some elderly Dublin tourists out for a walk, who were brimming with optimism about the future and offered a rather different assessment of the current climate: 'Look, the country has been through a rough time,' said one of the men with the air of someone used to public speaking. 'But nobody died. There's too much moaning and crying about it all. The economy is starting to grow again. Before we know it, we'll be back to where we were – if we make the right decisions.'

I thanked the man for his time, but nevertheless found it difficult to digest his view as I walked away. There were elements of truth in his view, I thought, but it didn't seem to acknowledge the full reality of people's lives. What about recession-related suicides, people losing their homes, and mass emigration? Was there too much moaning, or was there instead a legitimate cry that wasn't being heard? Arriving at the summit of a nearby hilltop, I reflected on this uncomfortable dimension of listening that I had previously avoided. If I was going to hear people's stories, I would inevitably come face-to-face with some perspectives that challenged my own. It was important not to be stuck in my own bubble – to get out, listen and keep an open mind.

I sat in the afternoon sunshine looking out on Inishbofin, sifting through my thoughts while taking in the beauty of the hilly green island. This was heaven, a far cry from last night's howling wind and rain, and a world away from the city life I had become accustomed to. But it was a bittersweet heaven. *What good is an island paradise if doesn't offer a future to its children?* I wondered. It was a question for Inishbofin and for Ireland as a whole.

Turning these questions over in my mind, I began to wander back towards the hostel, pausing to say hello to two men taking pictures by the roadside. The elder ran a small post office. He and his nephew, who had just graduated from university, were stopping off on Inishbofin as part of a west-coast boat trip. I know little about sailing but had long assumed it was the preserve of the rich and famous. The postmaster offered a different view. 'We sailed here on just a few euros' worth of fuel,' he said. 'We sleep on the boat and make our own meals, so it's all pretty cheap when you compare it with other types of holidays. The whole thing is about enjoying nature and seeing our beautiful country. It's really about tuning back into the simple things, the things that matter. Hope, for me, can be achieved by living a simple life,' he offered in response to my question. 'Forget the smartphones and all that – it's all about simplicity.'

Here it was again: that idea of simplicity as a seemingly vital ingredient to finding fulfilment. After a period of stress and severe burnout, I had finally started to discover that truth in my own life. But somehow I found myself distracted and busy once more, tangled up in an endless to-do list. Being on the road was giving me a chance to see clearly, to declutter and remember what really mattered.

The man's nephew chipped in, keen to give his view on the pair's sailing expedition: 'Yeah, it's unreal. It really makes you think about life. It's been really good for my head after all the stresses of college and finishing my exams, and wondering what to do now with the job situation. It just helps you get clarity and look at the world in a different way.' *What an inspiring time for this young man*, I thought. At a major juncture, he had his uncle's support through a kind of rite of passage as he prepared for the next stage of his life's journey.

———

Stepping inside Marie Coyne's seafront cottage, I felt as though history had come to life. Books, photos and precious family artifacts, including a pair of shoelaces used by her cobbler grandfather, adorned every surface.

Several people had urged me to pay Marie a visit. A passionate local historian, she carried much of Inishbofin's recent history in her own tale. She was 12 years old when electricity had first arrived on the island, and had witnessed other sweeping changes in her early life. For some reason I imagined her to be a sage-like older woman sitting beside a fire, ready to share her vast wisdom. But this remarkable islander, who left school at the age of 14, turned out to be a youthful-looking woman in her forties. 'I'd love to chat, Ruairí,' said Marie after I explained who I was and what I was up to. 'Come on in and I'll put the kettle on.'

Over a ritual several cups of tea, Marie recounted her childhood memories and described how Inishbofin had adjusted to modernity. 'I've always been a person fixated with the past. I did my homework by gaslight or candlelight. I remember lots of visiting going on. My grandmother's friends would come to visit her. They'd be chatting away, and I'd be listening in – so our house was always a bit chaotic, like a drop-in centre, with the post office on one side and the church on the other.

'When running water arrived in the early 1970s, it was huge. Before that, we had to go to the well for water. But the whole Celtic Tiger era never got here, so it hasn't changed that much. My mum said that people in times past wouldn't buy a new tin bucket unless they could pay for it. I do feel some people were foolish to a certain degree during the boom, but the banks were just feeding them and throwing everything at them – that wasn't right either,' she posited.

Marie's annual island headcount had registered a significant population decrease in recent years. But she was far from pessimistic about its future. 'Maybe it'll bounce back – perhaps people will move here or return from abroad. One young person who gives me great hope is my six-year-old niece, Ruby, who has Down's syndrome. Sometimes, when I'm not in the best of form, she can click me back. She's like a ray of sunshine, and she's very clued in. I get a lot of hope from Ruby.'

When I left Marie an hour later, I felt I had tapped into the true spirit of the island. She had abandoned her plans for the day to open her door and heart to a stranger, offering insights, stories, and kindness. It was a richness money could never buy.

———

Back at the hostel, I settled down for the magnificent dinner Brendan had proposed earlier this morning, though at this point it felt like it had been days. I listened to the chatter of guests from around the world as we sat together sharing stories in the soft candlelight while enjoying fresh fish, wine and the company of new friends.

I stayed up late listening, talking, and helping to clear up. By 1am, people headed for bed, but I felt simultaneously exhausted and wide awake. I had been up almost 20 hours, yet my mind was racing. There was so much I wanted to process, so I opened my laptop and uploaded some blogs, photos and audio to share with the growing number of people who had taken an interest in my trip. It was after 2.30am when I climbed back into my tent, and I needed to be up around 7am to catch the first ferry back to Cleggan. So much for learning to live the simple life!

'Throw your rucksack on the back,' Brendan said the next morning when he turned up with a mountain bike to help transport my luggage. 'This is the VIP treatment. You can't say we don't look after people here, Ruairí.' As we proceeded down the hill towards the ferry, I felt a little sad to be saying goodbye. During the short stay I had made so many new friends on Inishbofin. This was clearly the sort of place you could come to visit and find yourself still there decades later, much like Jesús did in Spiddal. But I had more places to explore and stories to hear.

'So, you're finally off,' said a voice behind me as the ferry set sail. It was Adrian, owner of the Beach Bar, where I had stopped before dinner the night before. Adrian had learned about my trip on Twitter and invited me to visit him at the pub, restaurant and bed and breakfast that he ran with his partner Órla. He had initially moved to Inishbofin from Loughrea, a mainland town about three hours away, to be with her.

'People are looking for something different, a better standard of food and experience, so that's what we aim to do with the Beach Bar,' he said. 'We have to invest in better service, in locally sourced organic food and drink. I think it's vital that we produce more food locally, which will encourage job creation and help us secure a more sustainable future here on the island,' he added with conviction.

Adrian was headed to the mainland for supplies. 'I heard you were looking for Damien Dempsey,' he remarked. 'Did you meet him in the end?'

'No, I didn't, but I'm sure it just wasn't meant to be,' I replied, trying to remain upbeat. 'He's in the Beach Bar right now,' Adrian said. 'I just left him – he was playing music there last night.' I couldn't believe what I was hearing. 'Pity you missed him. He's a total legend, isn't he? I love him. He does a huge amount for young people and the wider community. Why not come back with me on the return leg and I'll introduce you?'

'I don't think so, Adrian, but thank you,' I replied. 'I've tried in vain to meet him, so now I need to let it go. Besides, I need to keep the show on the road.' The sun beamed down on us as we made our way across the Atlantic to Cleggan. I started to think about where I would head next, but my mind kept drifting back to Adrian's proposal. Maybe it was meant to be after all. Perhaps this was the next twist in the story. Returning to the island in the same day seemed a bit ridiculous, but perhaps it was just mad enough to work. After all, at the heart of this trip was the freedom to go wherever the wind blew me.

'Ah, feck it,' I found myself saying to Adrian, 'I'll come back with ya later.' We both laughed. After a few hours on the mainland, I found myself sailing into Inishbofin Harbour, only to spot Brendan, Róisín and her mother, who were there to see off some friends. Brendan shook his head in disbelief, laughing as if to say, 'What kind of idiot have we got on our hands?' The poor fella was probably starting to wonder if he'd have to make my breakfast every morning now.

The harbour was busy with people waiting to board the return ferry to Cleggan. Among them was a guy I recognised from Dublin, Dean Scurry, whom I had met through community work. 'Ah, Inishbofin – the land of the Irish spirits,' he replied with a big grin when I asked what he was up to on the island. 'I'm here with me mates for a few days – a bit of walking, chilling, eating, drinking, chatting the heads off each other. It's a great place to turn off all the bullshit in your head, get back to nature.' Dean was a youth worker in Ballymun, a densely populated part of Dublin that had suffered its fair share of hardships. He was also an activist who discerned the clear connection between his community's suffering and wider, systemic inequalities.

'We've been through the most awful period of indulgence in our history, from what I can see,' said Dean. 'It's time to take a step back from that and get back to what I had when I was a kid: community. We need to start looking at our rights, talking to each other and focusing on love and truth rather than backhandedness and greed. I'm not focusing on the negative stuff anymore. I've had enough of that.'

By the time we finished talking, the boat to Cleggan was set to depart, and Dean had to hurry up and jump on board. 'Give me a call when you get back to Dublin!' he shouted. I wandered back over to Adrian, who was talking with some friends. 'So, how did you get on with Damo?' Adrian asked once the ferry had left. 'What do you mean?' I asked, baffled. 'Are you joking me? Damien Dempsey was standing right beside you just 60 seconds ago!' he said. 'Right beside you. I assumed you would end up chatting with him.' He pointed towards the ferry that was slowly chugging out of the harbour. 'Look over there at the boat. See that big guy at the back? That's him.'

I put my head in my hands and groaned deeply. 'I don't believe this!' I sighed, as Adrian, Brendan, Róisín and her mother stood laughing as the ferry disappeared out to sea.

4

The Wolf You Feed

Maam Cross to Westport

'SO, HOW DID YOU DECIDE TO COME TO BOFIN?' I ASKED
Tony, a cheery man from Cork who had offered me a lift during my
final ferry ride from Inishbofin earlier that morning. I had taken Róisín
and her mother up on their offer to stay on the island one more night.

'There was a big gang of us there, most of us involved in music,' he
replied. 'I used to organise gigs for Damien Dempsey and he was with
us, so it was a chance to catch up with him as well. We had a great time
together eating good food, playing tunes and jumping off the pier.'

This was getting ridiculous. I had seen men jumping off the pier during my time on Inishbofin and even took a photo of them, albeit from
a distance. Perhaps I now even had a photo of Damo. 'Damo and the
others headed off yesterday on the ferry. We decided to stay the extra
night,' he said. I nodded and smiled to myself, deciding not to recount
my story. It was time to let it go or run the risk of meeting Damo in
years to come and facing the question: 'Are you that weirdo who was
chasing me around Inishbofin?'

On we travelled through the Connemara boglands, lakes and
mountains, our conversation winding with the road, discussing the
state of the music industry and how grateful we felt to live in such a

beautiful country. Before I knew it, we were entering Maam Cross, and the thought suddenly dawned on me that I was slightly off course. Earlier that morning, I had decided it was probably best to head somewhat northerly, but I got so caught up in the conversation with Tony that I hadn't noticed the turn-off in that direction 20 minutes earlier. Slightly annoyed with myself, I thanked my new friend and hopped out to see what was in store.

Maam Cross, a regional crossroads situated in the middle of nowhere, contained little more than a hotel and a livestock mart. But as luck would have it, the place was buzzing like a rural mecca in the heart of a natural wilderness. It was Mart Day. Not far from the hotel stood the giant, steel-framed market building, from which sheep and cows cried out, filling the air with echoes of their disquiet. Nearby was a boarded-up petrol station and shop, a remnant of better days in this area. On each side of the road, hardy-looking men gathered in groups beside mart stalls selling everything from fast food and live chickens to chainsaws and work clothes.

I had been living in the city for a long time, yet I knew this world well. My grandfather Dan was a part-time farmer, and I had grown up next to a farm where I helped out on occasion. Bizarrely, the smell of fresh cow dung still evokes warm nostalgia in me. Despite this familiarity, I somehow felt out of place here; perhaps city life had softened me up and distanced me from my rustic, rural roots.

Rain began to pelt down on the weather-beaten men and animals. I suspected these farmers might not take too kindly to a stranger hanging around asking questions, but this felt like a rare chance to delve into a world far removed from my life in the city; to learn from people whose voices are rarely heard in the national media, despite their importance to Ireland's economic and cultural fabric. This was Ireland's Wild West, a place where the old ways still held sway. With some trepidation, I ventured towards the mart building where animals were being sold as they had been for generations. Once inside, I couldn't help feeling like a spy, or at least a journalist, here to poke my potentially unwelcome nose around. My nervousness wasn't helped by the cries that echoed throughout the building from hundreds of fearful-looking animals.

I wandered around trying to look relaxed, as if I was there on business or to meet a friend. Men stood shoulder-to-shoulder, looking in on their animals while chatting in Irish and English about things I couldn't understand, regardless of the language. Finally, like a swimmer on a diving board, I held my breath and jumped in. 'What? Hope? Hope for Ireland!' growled the first man I approached, whose tired eyes, wrinkles and grey hair put him in his late fifties. 'There's no hope for Ireland. This country is fecked. It's over. It's finished.' And with that he walked off, leaving me in the dust of his rage. It seemed my apprehension had been justified. I was stung by the man's pent-up anger, which he had shot out like a verbal bullet.

I picked myself up and resolved to try again as I continued to stroll past large huddles of men and animals bleating from their cramped pens. I lingered near a middle-aged man who was leaning against a wall, talking on his mobile phone. After he finished his call, I approached. He didn't hold back. 'We need a revolution,' the man responded when I asked him about Ireland's future. 'We've been betrayed, sold off to Brussels. The free Irishman has become a thing of the past. Fishing, farming, hunting, working in the bog, they're all being killed off. The big political parties, they all seem like they're part of the same machine, robbing the Irish people of our resources and handing them to their friends.

'I lived in England years ago,' he continued, 'and I probably should have stayed there. In England, they value the working man. They haven't sold out their own people the same way we have,' he said, his fist clenching. 'This isn't a political game. People are killing themselves. We are losing more and more of our people to suicide because of these policies. I know one young farmer who recently shot dead all his cattle and then himself. As far as I can see, a lot of this isn't being reported in the media, which seems to be centered mainly around what happens in Dublin.'

I was speechless. While I had read numerous reports on men's health, rural life, and Ireland's high suicide rate, this emotional testimony transformed them into something all the more real. I wondered how a man like this stayed sane, how he woke up every day and got on with things. 'You just have to,' he replied, with a serious look on his face. 'For your family, for your kids. What other choice do I have?' Suddenly he calmed, his voice grew softer, and a peaceful look spread over his face. 'Also, the music – the music helps. I play traditional Irish music, the concertina, and the warmth and spirit of the music lifts my spirits and brings us all together, away from all the crap. There's something in the music, in the camaraderie, that's a great antidote to all the other shite.'

Before I knew it, he was gone, whisked into the bustle of the mart. I was left standing there, unable to digest all that he had shared, but turning one phrase over in my mind. 'Something in the music', he had said. I liked that.

Within seconds, I made eye contact with a younger farmer whom I had briefly greeted earlier. He had kind eyes that made him easy to approach. 'No, I don't mind talking at all,' he said. 'It's a strange day for me. I'm here with my brother selling the last of his animals.' He had worked in construction and farming for most of his life. Many of his friends had emigrated, he said, and he too was out of work and facing pressure to leave. He had separated from his wife, and his children were the only things stopping him from emigrating. 'It would break my heart to leave them. I feel trapped, and there's no easy way out. My eldest has already started talking about emigrating. That's how bad things are around here,' he said, with such emotion that I thought he was going to cry.

My heart went out to him at that moment. I wanted to empty my pockets and give him whatever money I had, to hug him and tell him to keep going. He could probably have done with the hug, but I couldn't bring myself to offer it against the powerful inhibitions wrought by cultural and social conditioning. Reluctant to leave him without at least offering some support, I asked how he was coping. 'It's hard, to be honest. I might not be able to cope if it wasn't for the antidepressants. But really it comes down to my children – I want to to be there for them. I know it sounds a bit corny, but I get hope from my children and my love for them.'

I hadn't expected him to share such a harrowing tale, but I detected in him a strength that assured me he'd be okay. That he had something to hold on to, a love to keep him going, was positive. And equally as important, he was able to open up and articulate his situation. I thought back to the social conditioning that had deterred my hug. I had seen time and again how cultural norms around masculinity prevented men, including myself, from communicating and expressing ourselves in healthy ways. The 'boys don't cry' fallacy is a travesty that has caused too much hurt. If this young farmer was barely hanging on, I could only imagine how tough it must be for those who keep their pain bottled up, who attempt to drink it away and who find themselves willing to end their own lives. Fathers who are separated from their children, as this farmer might end up, are particularly affected – I had met several over the years. I found myself thinking too of the pain of emigration; of all those who had left Ireland over the centuries for Boston, Chicago, Liverpool and Melbourne. What hardships, sorrows and regrets had they taken with them? Emigrant successes are often well documented, but I wondered about the others: the drinkers in Philadelphia and the homeless in London. I thought of all the stories that will remain untold, all the people who might never find words to express their devastation.

I told the man that I could see he was an amazing father, and I suspected the future would bring good things for him. My heart was heavy as I prepared to leave Maam Cross, but I took comfort in the great strength amid adversity I had observed in the men at the mart. It felt like an ancient strength – one that had carried their ancestors through even harder times. There was a dignity in these men, a fierce love of the land and a sense of community that suggested they would stand firm against the rush towards so-called progress.

I decided to head north towards Leenane, a picturesque village on the Galway-Mayo border, and take things from there. That was the plan, at least. Half an hour later I was soaking wet from the rain, realising that the chances of a lift on a road with no traffic were pretty slim. I backtracked and chanced my luck with the R344, an alternative route that cuts through the heart of Connemara. I was just making myself comfortable in my new hitching spot when a couple in a small red car pulled up and offered me a lift. I jumped inside, grateful to be out of the rain and curious about my temporary hosts. 'We're on our way to a camping trip with our friends,' the young woman in the passenger seat said with a strong Polish accent.

'Yes, great camping weather, as you can see,' joked her boyfriend.

'I like it here a lot,' the woman remarked. 'Ireland is so beautiful, and people really are friendly. Well, most people are,' she added. 'But you know, I don't think about politics and the future and all of that too much. I just do my job as a waitress, meet my friends, and try to enjoy things. I try to keep things simple. So I am probably not a good person to talk to for your trip,' she concluded. That only encouraged me. I believe everyone has wisdom to share and stories to tell, so I wasn't going to let her get away that easily.

Sure enough, she was a qualified psychologist with an interesting perspective on the human mind: 'As I said, I like to keep things simple. Life doesn't need to be so complicated. So much of the negativity around is from watching the news and believing too much that politics is the reality. I know it is important, but it's not the total reality. Reality is whatever you make it for yourself. It's like that story of the two wolves – you know the one?' she asked. I told her I wasn't familiar. 'It's an old Cherokee story,' she said. 'A grandparent is telling their grandchild that there are two wolves fighting for control of our minds. One is filled with fear, envy, greed, anger and hate. The other is loving, kind, humble, peace-loving and generous. The grandchild becomes worried and wants to know which wolf is going to win. The grandparent says, 'The one that will win is the one that you feed.'

Far from not having anything to say, this woman had shared one of the most powerful stories I had heard so far – one I wished the entire nation could hear. 'That myth sums up so much for me,' she ended. 'There's a battle for our minds, from within and without, and ultimately it's up to us to be clear about our response to that.'

———

The rain had cleared when I finally reached Leenane, and Killary Fjord dazzled in the warm evening sun. This was the Ireland of postcards:

a small, rural village hugged by mountains, set beside the water, and possibly containing more sheep than humans. Leenane had served as the filming location for *The Quiet Man*, the classic 1952 movie starring John Wayne and Maureen O'Hara.

I decided to pop into a nearby pub to find a quiet corner to give my fiancée Susan a call. Stepping into the pub was like setting foot inside another reality: a room full of drunk men who were singing, shouting, falling around and – mostly – enjoying themselves. Tourists pretended to study their guidebooks while furtively looking on, trying to make sense of this scene. I guessed the revellers had been to the mart at Maam Cross earlier and were busy drinking away some of the hard-earned proceeds of their sales. I ordered a drink, found a spot in the corner I thought wouldn't be as hectic, then took out my phone. I hoped I'd be able to hear Susan amid the shouts and screeches. 'Hey, you! Yeah, you with the phone,' growled a small, drunken man as my hope quickly evaporated. 'Are you out walking, or what are you at?' he shouted, pointing at my rucksack.

'No, I'm hitching around Ireland and just stopping off to make a call,' I replied, hoping this would satisfy my uninvited inquisitor.

'Hitching? Ah, good luck with that,' he fired back, tacking on an angry slur that I recognised immediately for the drunken talk it was. I decided I had no time for his aggressive edge, noting that conversations such as these tend not to go anywhere useful.

'I'll chat with you later, I'm just going to make a phone call here,' I said, letting him know I wasn't going to humour him. 'Ah well, feck ya then. Go make your feckin' phone call, ya bollox ya,' came his not-so-diplomatic response, to our onlookers' bemusement.

All I could do was smile and shrug. Just my luck – I was only looking to make a call. At a table beside me, four tourists looked over in sympathy and solidarity. 'That's the way it sometimes goes, especially with the drink,' one of them said in a northern accent as he sipped a creamy pint of stout. The group, an older couple and their son and daughter-in-law, were stopping off in Leenane as part of a two-week holiday in the west.

'We love the west coast, the open spaces and fresh air. It's hard to beat. Great for the head,' the older woman said, explaining that while she and her husband were well into their seventies, they were still very active and enjoying life.

'Being down here, I haven't been online and only get the odd text message,' her daughter-in-law added. 'At home, you're on the go, your brain is occupied all the time. Whereas down here, you don't have a choice – you can't charge around the place. It's a much slower pace of life.'

The father had lived quite a life. Formerly a successful businessman, he described how he had been extorted and threatened by paramilitaries during the 30 years of political violence in the north. At one point, he said, he was forced to flee the country for safety – something not uncommon when people refused to play ball with the militarised groups in the north. 'If you told a ten-year-old now what it was like back then, they wouldn't believe you. But it was still a good place to be brought up,' he said.

This family had clearly been through a lot, as had so many people during the conflict in the north. Often known as 'The Troubles' – a name that perhaps doesn't do justice to the extent of the suffering – the period between the late 1960s and the late 1990s saw over 3,000 people killed and almost 50,000 injured. Bombings, beatings and other forms of violence massively disrupted daily life. What was often viewed from outside as a religious conflict between Catholics and Protestants was more accurately a conflict over identity, allegiance and rights. Northern Ireland had been sectioned off as part of the United Kingdom since 1922. Although identities were rapidly shifting, the majority of Catholics were native to the region and often referred to as Republicans or Nationalists. They generally identified as Irish, and most wanted a reunited Ireland. The majority of Protestants, commonly of Scottish or English heritage, were traditionally seen as British Unionists who wanted Northern Ireland to remain part of the United Kingdom, though this is changing.

While tensions had existed for centuries between these two tribes, there had been a relatively stable period of peace in the decades prior to the 1960s. In the late 1960s, however, Nationalist civil rights protests demanded an end to discrimination in housing and employment, as well as voting rights for the Catholic minority. The protests were met with suppression. The British government deployed troops, triggering the onset of violence, the formation of various paramilitary groups and three decades of horror.

Growing up less than 30 kilometres south of the border, I had felt the conflict in the air during my childhood. Like most people on the southern side, my family wasn't directly affected by the violence. However, it was hard to forget that there were bombs going off just a few kilometres up the road. I have vivid memories of young soldiers with machine guns peering in the back of our family car as we crossed military checkpoints on trips to visit my mother's family in Donegal. As teenagers, my pals and I often succumbed to foolish prejudices: we talked about 'prods' and 'orange bastards', and sang rebel songs with older men in the local pubs.

The ignorance of my teens ended when I went to university in Scotland and for the first time got to know people of different backgrounds. Catholics and Protestants, Nationalists and Unionists, Republicans and Loyalists, all identity labels for two communities with so much in common. It didn't take us long to realise that the main borders were in people's minds, and that the biggest enemy we faced was the segregation that had prevented us getting to know each other.

'In the Northern Ireland I remember, everyone got on very well,' the man continued, 'and then the so-called Troubles came, and people who had been friendly started to believe that each other were the opposition, the other side. Things are very different now, and hopefully, it'll keep improving. The people on both sides are good. When politicians realise their responsibility to unite us as one community, not as two separate communities, nothing but good will come.'

The volume of his voice increased as he turned his attention to the banking industry. 'We grew up with the belief that you got out of life what you put in. Unfortunately, the bankers disproved that – the regulations were ripped up, and greed took over. Now, all our savings and our pensions are gone, along with large sums of money meant for our children. Instead of having plenty of money, we're left frightened to spend what we do have. So I hold bankers in complete and utter contempt – and I come from a banking background. I think what they did was a criminal act; those who engaged in it should be pursued in the courts,' the man added with indignance. But despite the many struggles this man had faced, he seemed to exude a sense of calm and inner peace, which he attributed to a sense of faith. 'Spirituality will secure you and support you and take you through life,' he said on a final, hopeful note.

I thanked the family for their time and explained that I really needed to go and call Susan back. I had promised her an hour ago that I was going to call back right away, but I hadn't expected to fend off a potential bar fight or stumble into conversation with a former banker on the topic of troubles with paramilitaries.

———

Soon after leaving the pub, I was sitting in a van on my way to Westport, 32 kilometres north of Leenane. 'You're joking me,' I said to Des, a butcher from Clifden who had picked me up. To my surprise, he had already heard about my trip. Adrian from Inishbofin had been on his way to the mainland to pick up supplies from none other than Des when I bumped into him on the ferry and got talking about Damo. 'Small world indeed,' said Des. 'I only heard about you and what you are up to, and now here I am giving you a lift the very next day. What are the chances?'

Des explained the change he'd noticed in Ireland after he'd returned from living in England for some time. 'When I came home from England, I found that people weren't able to stand up for themselves. People were proud before, but now they're all yes-men,' he railed. 'They're led astray by Europe. I have no faith in politics, not a bit. Once they get in, they carry on and do what the crowd before them were doing. Look at the state of the infrastructure. If we had a good, high-speed broadband in the west we could create jobs and nobody would have to leave. It's a crazy situation.' His passionate political views were matched by his passion for food, and his belief in Ireland's potential as a global food hub – if only small farmers and producers were given a fair chance and not squeezed out by global chains. 'We have the big supermarkets throwing stuff out the door at any price, and it's very hard to compete. We have better quality, but that doesn't say anything anymore. Plus, many people can't afford it because they don't have the money,' he added. 'You can't blame them. They're not getting the same quality, but still, it's going to keep them fed'.

'We've got a great future because we have the best food.' He spoke with pride. 'There's no country in the world with beef and lamb like it. We could be the best country in the world, if only we had the weather,' he said, jokingly, as we arrived into Westport.

———

The next day I awoke in a bed and breakfast, rested and ready for action. Sunlight streamed through my bedroom window, dropping sparkles of light on the bed. Croagh Patrick, Ireland's most famous mountain, was calling me. I ventured downstairs into the dining area, where a large, red-faced man was sweating as he served the guests giant plates of sausages, bacon, eggs, toast and black pudding. I looked on, filled with a mix of horror and temptation. I could cope with the grease factor, but I couldn't help but remember the pained cries of the animals at the Maam Cross mart. Then again, there was Des the butcher and the need to support small farmers and businesses. It was too early for this ethical debate, and minutes later, I was devouring my full Irish breakfast.

I figured the two women seated next to me, both Irish and seemingly in their late forties, were either on their way to or from Sunday mass. My preconceived notions were soon banished when they told me what they were up to. 'We're just back from Achill Island,' said one of them – a red-headed woman with big blue eyes. 'We were on a retreat there, and we're heading back south soon.'

'What kind of retreat, if you don't mind me asking?'

She cleared her throat, perhaps wary of sharing. 'Well, it was run by a Jewish woman from New York, but it was essentially a Shamanic retreat where we looked at things like shadow work, spirit guides and past lives. I'm not sure if that makes any sense to you?' It was definitely not your average Sunday morning chat in rural Ireland. Then again, I wasn't surprised. I had met many people who were disillusioned with organised religion and looking for deeper ways of connecting without abandoning spirituality altogether.

Filled to content after my massive breakfast, I decided to stroll around Westport before hitching out to Croagh Patrick, or the Reek, as it's known locally. Westport is one of Ireland's few planned towns, notable for its historic buildings and orderly streets. The shopfronts sparkled in the morning sun as tourists and locals exchanged good wishes for the day ahead. Down near the Carrowbeg river I passed St. Mary's Church and streams of worshippers flocking to Sunday mass. Outside the church was a memorial to John MacBride, a local revolutionary executed by the British government for his role in the 1916 Easter Rising.

On the memorial was a quote from MacBride that read: 'No man can claim authority to barter away the immutable rights of Nationhood; for Irishmen have fought, suffered, and died in defence of those rights. And, thank God, Irishmen will always be found to snatch up the torch from the slumbering fire, to hold it aloft as a guiding light, and to hand it on, blazing afresh, to the succeeding generation.'

Though I existed in a different time and set of circumstances than MacBride, as I read his words I considered what it might mean to carry the torch forward in today's world. While the rights of nationhood are important, it seems that problems like the ecological crisis on our planet require us to think beyond the nation-state. Perhaps the torch that needs to be carried now is more of a global one – a light strong enough to drown out the darkness and division that is causing so much despair. There was plenty to ponder as I set off to climb the sacred mountain.

5

Lugh's Mountain

Croagh Patrick to Newport

AT JUST 764 METRES, THE REEK ISN'T THAT HIGH BY
international standards. But in Irish terms, it's a mountain of iconic
stature. It has been a focal point for pilgrims for thousands of years and
holds a special place in the hearts of many Irish people. Each year, on the
last Sunday of July, anywhere from 15,000 to 30,000 people make their
way up its craggy slopes, many of them barefoot. These days, the pilgrimage honours the Christian missionary Patrick, one of the patron saints
of Ireland – the other being Brigid. But in earlier times, the ritual 'Reek
Sunday' climb coincided with the ancient Irish harvest festival of Lugh-
nasa and paid homage to a different hero: Lugh, god of the sun. He was
a pretty big deal back then. Prior to the advent of electricity, the sun was
everything – source of food and fuel, giver of life. It was a fierce quest for
survival that can be hard to comprehend in today's world; the connection
to this provider mattered greatly. It made sense then that Croagh Patrick
was said to have been called 'Lugh's Mountain' before its christening.

The traditional pilgrimage date was still weeks away, but I thought
it would be apt to take a pause in my trip, make the trek, and let myself
sink into the gratitude I was feeling. Things were flowing – from the
hitchhiking and weather, to money and accommodation. How freeing

to be out on the road like this, rediscovering my country, with time and space to listen, learn, and share. I had a lot to be grateful for – not only this trip, but also the love in my life, my health and the huge opportunities ahead. Too often, I had chosen to see the gaps and succumb to a cycle of negativity that was holding me back. As the Polish woman explained, I had perhaps overly fed the wolf of despair.

———

I had barely stuck out my thumb for a lift on the scenic R335 to Lugh's Mountain when a woman with warm, smiling eyes pulled up in a camper van and told me to hop in. 'I used to hitch years ago,' she reminisced, beaming with excitement after hearing what I was up to. 'I went all over the place and had the best of times. People can be a bit brainwashed these days,' she remarked with a sudden shift in tone. 'We've been sold a lie about how to live and how to behave. It's all about playing it safe, hiding in your own little corner.' I recalled my own internal debate before embarking on this journey, the pull to stay in my job simply because it seemed reckless to do something different.

'It's all nonsense,' she asserted in a strong midlands accent. 'It's a myth. Heaven isn't up there in the sky waiting for you when you die. It's here, right now – this is it. Heaven is right here on Earth, we're living it, but we're doing a damn fine job of turning it into hell.'

We travelled along the coastal road, the view of Croagh Patrick emerging to my left as fishing boats and kayaks moved gently through the clear blue waters of Clew Bay to my right.

'Your trip is about hope?' she asked. 'If you ask me, hope is something you have to find in yourself, in your own heart, your own mind.' The story she told me next put this idea into sobering context. 'Years ago,' she began, 'when I was young, my brother was killed in a hit-and-run by men on their way home from the pub. I learned later that someone witnessed men leaving the scene. She knew who they were. They were powerful figures in the area, and she told my parents. They were in shock and couldn't take it all in. When they did start asking questions, it was clear there was a cover-up, and that it was a battle they probably couldn't win. I was too young to know anything about it, and my parents were too grief-stricken to take on powerful people and institutions. They had no power or influence and had to find a way to cope. The truth has been buried in silence ever since.'

I was flabbergasted – although perhaps I shouldn't have been. There has been no shortage of revelations concerning corruption and abuses of power in Irish society. Charities, churches, businesses, the health system, sports associations, media, policing, politics – there are almost no sections of society that have been left unscathed. This woman's story, as shocking as it was, was not entirely out of context with some of the scandals that have emerged in recent years. In all of these, there prevailed a common theme of corruption, cover-ups and the silencing of those who aspired to shine a light. It was no wonder that a new wave of courageous whistleblowers and truth-tellers was starting to emerge.

Arriving at the foot of the Reek, the woman left me with some parting words: 'It's not easy, but I'm having to live with all of this and try to find a way of making sense of the world. It's hard living with a sense of injustice, and it has taken a huge toll on my family. I've realised that I can't carry all that. I deserve to be happy, and I'm focused on that. So you want my views on hope? Don't rely on the world to give you hope. We have to make hope from the raw materials we are given, as rough as they might be.'

———

At the foot of the Reek, the woman's story still rolling through my mind, I looked up at the mountain's steep, rocky slope as the sun poured rays upon the hundreds of people on their way up and down. Observing the peak, memories flooded back from the last time I had been here, a few years previously. I had a camper van at the time, and the perfect partner to join me on my ascent: a small wooden sculpture of Lugh. It had been carved by Sligo's renowned storyteller and craftsman Michael Quirke and was a gift from my mother. For a bit of a laugh, I had gone so far as to secure Lugh's small wooden body – all 30 centimetres of it – beneath the passenger seat belt as I set off in the van. Saint Patrick was getting all the love around here, and I figured it was time to bring the main man back. At the foot of the mountain, the two legends came head-to-head. There stood a towering statue of Patrick, with a giant staff in his hand and a determined look on his face. Meanwhile, Lugh was sitting pretty in my rucksack, head peeking out, surveying the land. 'Time you took your mountain back,' I said to Lugh, smiling as I sat him up beside Patrick for a photo.

The foot of the mountain was bustling with tourists and pilgrims. Excitement and fraternity filled the summer air as those descending the mountain offered words of encouragement to those of us who were arriving. It was mostly an older crowd, along with a few young folk from the traditionally itinerant Travelling community, a recognised Irish ethnic group of approximately 30,000 people. Pilgrimages to the Reek are a big part of Travelling culture, as is Catholicism in general.

I wanted to talk to everyone, to find out who they were and what had brought them to the Reek. I decided to approach a woman who looked like she was about to set off on her ascent. 'No thanks – maybe it is better just to enjoy the walk,' she replied in a Dutch accent with a deadpan look on her face. That was me told. She was right, though. This listening project was about listening to my own voice as much as it was about listening to others. I needed some periods of quiet to look inward and enjoy the experience of the trip rather than overthink it.

I made my way upwards on a path that had seen countless soles, past a sparkling stream of fresh mountain water. Soon I reached the rockier, steeper part of the climb. As I progressed, I began to feel a certain expansiveness – the kind where your thoughts start to untangle, and you start to see the world from a broader perspective. I had always loved climbing mountains for this reason. I loved the struggle to the top, the periods of rest along the way, and the final, glorious view from the summit. When I hit the halfway point, I sat to rest, taking in the rugged majesty of Clew Bay and the hundreds of small islands and inlets dotting its sun-kissed waters. It felt good to be alive, looking out over one of the most beautiful places on Earth.

I was three-quarters of the way towards the summit when the going got tough, and I slowed to catch my breath. Several runners passed by with ease, doing nothing for my self-esteem, but the view was much sweeter in the slow lane. 'Some craic this, eh?' a man said through laboured breaths as he approached. The man was home from the United States, he told me. 'I've been there almost 30 years and I still love it, but it's good to get home,' he said. Like many Irish people in the US, he was involved in the pub trade and had done well, but he hadn't forgotten his roots. 'Gaelic football keeps me plugged into the Irish community. I'm involved in training young fellas, and it means I get to meet people from all over Ireland and stay connected. My kids were all born in the US, but they're involved in Gaelic sports too, and they love it,' he said proudly, in an accent that had faded little over the years.

'A great day for it!' he cheerfully remarked to every second person we met as we proceeded up the mountain. He seemed to know people from every county in Ireland, a legacy of his time welcoming young emigrants to the United States. 'So you're from Tipperary?' he would ask passers-by. 'Do you know Joey Murray or Peadar Ryan?' Sure enough, before long he would succeed in making a local connection. Our conversation moved on to politics, and my new hiking companion did not hold back. 'I'll tell ya, people down south, they need to stand up for themselves like we had to up north during the civil rights movement. Otherwise, you're going to keep getting walked all over. You don't get your rights unless you demand them.'

Here on the mountain, the spirit of camaraderie and community was tangible. We were all in it together, young and old, rich and poor, all carrying our hopes, dreams and fears to the summit. It was as if the mountain had stripped away the layers of identity and ego and brought us closer to our natural state, our true selves. *If only this spirit was more prevalent in the world*, I thought to myself.

Calls of 'Nearly there now!' and 'One last push!' from those on their way down made the final stretch easier. Suddenly, I was at the summit, on what felt like the top of the world, looking out on a spectacular panorama of mountains and sea, islands and nearby farms and villages. 'Ireland, you beauty,' I said out loud from a spot where tens of thousands had stood before me, experiencing a similar connection to something much bigger than themselves.

I ventured over to the edge of the barren rock and sat for a while, attempting a moment of meditation. My mind had just started to settle when I heard a hum rippling through the warm summer air. I thought for a minute. *Am I imagining this?* Had I tapped into some weird cosmic vortex? I listened harder and shook my head. This was bizarre. The sound kept coming, repetitive murmurs, rising and falling through the wind, hypnotic, captivating and intriguing. The sounds grew louder until, unable to contain my curiosity, I decided to go and find their source. On the other side of the expansive summit, I spotted a dozen pilgrims, aged between about 15 and 70 years old, chanting the rosary in unison. Their voices created waves of sound that transported me back to a time when my grandparents used to gather their rosary beads to recite this prayer. I'd heard it countless times before, but here on the mountain it somehow made sense to me for the first time.

In this form, it was a meditation, not unlike chants I had heard in India – a continuous drone of words imbued with intention, working bodies and minds into a state of calm. I was caught off guard, transfixed by the primal chant before my mind could kick in with analysis and judgment. I watched and listened, appreciating this communal ritual that no app or gadget could replace. How much longer would we see scenes like this, as Irish society changed at breakneck speed? Was I witnessing the last gasp of a tradition, here on this mountain of memories?

———

'There's no doubt that this mountain is a special place,' said Lorcan, a man who had taken a seat on the rock beside me to finish his lunch. 'I don't think of myself as very spiritual, but I suppose it's a spiritual thing and a tourist thing too. It's a great day out. I did it as a young lad back in the 1970s – it was like a rite of passage.' I asked Lorcan if he had a vision for Ireland. 'I lost my job a year ago, so my vision is that I'd like to be back working again, but not at what I was doing before,' he told me. 'We've come through the Celtic Tiger years, and I suppose as a country we're recognising we lost a bit of our soul. We're finding that again, and I think it's a good opportunity for people to look inward.

'You can see the spirit of people wanting to help each other here today on the mountain,' he continued. 'That's an Irish thing, it's in our culture. We need to recognise that we're good communicators and we get on with people. We see the lame duck and we always help them.' When I asked how he had coped with unemployment, his response reminded me of Adrian in Inishbofin and Adrian's butcher, Des. 'I went back to college and got new expertise in culinary arts,' Lorcan revealed. 'I've always been interested in food. This is a food island, and that needs to be encouraged. We might need to shop at cheap supermarkets, but that doesn't mean we can't treat ourselves to artisan, handmade food. If you look at France, Italy or Spain, you see street markets with local produce and freshly cooked food. We shouldn't be insular – we need to encourage ourselves to do better.'

It made sense, this food vision. Ireland is one of the planet's greenest, most fertile islands, and remains mostly free from genetically modified crops. With our natural resources, it makes no sense that we import much of our food, bringing in potatoes from England and Israel and apples and lamb from New Zealand while simultaneously exporting our own. If we invested more in promoting local food production and consumption, we could reduce carbon emissions, save money, create tens of thousands of jobs and perhaps give new hope to young people and farmers like those I had met at the animal mart in Connemara. It could also be an opportunity to move away from the fast-food culture that contributes to high levels of disease and an overstretched health service. People like Lorcan recognised Ireland's potential to become a global beacon for healthy and sustainable food and farming, and indeed would be critical to its success. I wished him success and left the summit, beginning my descent.

'You're nearly there now,' I said on my way down to the weary-looking souls trudging in the opposite direction, repaying the motivational exchanges I had benefited from just an hour earlier. I found myself walking next to a retired man in his sixties and one of the chanters from the summit. It turned out that he and his church parish group were on one of their regular outings.

'It's a way of getting out and about and socialising,' he told me. 'We're also involved in community development, especially welcoming newcomers to the area.' I was curious to hear what he thought about some of the criticisms of the Church. 'Well, my son is a priest who has served as a missionary in Africa,' he replied, 'and I know from him and others that there are good people in the Church. It's like any institution: there are good and bad, especially when an organisation becomes that big.' It was true, I thought. Though I had always maintained that an organisation claiming moral supremacy should be held to the highest standards.

The man told me how witnessing extreme poverty as a young teacher in Dublin had left a lasting impression on him, opening his eyes to inequality and leading him into decades of community service. 'My blood boils when I see all the injustice in this country, especially the corruption tribunals that end up costing millions and telling us nothing.' Nevertheless, he seemed to be enjoying life and embracing the freedom of retirement. 'I admire your idealism and enthusiasm,' he told me as we prepared to part ways at the foot of the mountain. We shook hands, and before I knew it, he had slipped me a €20 note and bolted off. 'It's towards your journey! Enjoy every second!' he shouted.

———

A few hours later, after an easy lift with a young couple back into Westport, I stood on the side of the road once again. But this time, I cursed myself for a lack of foresight – the roads in rural Ireland tend to be extremely quiet on Sunday evenings. My aunt Rosaleen lived just 20 minutes away in Newport, and I was long overdue for a visit. Another half hour went by, and still no lift. Susan phoned as I was starting to feel frustrated, and I told her the situation. She encouraged me to get a taxi, as it was only a short trip. 'No, I can't,' I said, looking across the road to where a taxi had parked up. 'It's a hitching trip, so I need to stick it out. I can't be wasting money on taxis.'

'You might not want to waste money, but you're also wasting time that you could be spending with your aunt,' she replied with her typical graceful wisdom. 'Besides, people have given you money to help out with your trip, so just use it to support the trip – simple.' I have a tendency to do things the hard way, and I knew she was right. I shouted across to the taxi driver, who had his window down. 'How much for a lift to Newport?'

'Between €15 and €20,' came the reply, 'but I'll do it for a tenner.' Minutes later, I was on my way to Newport, listening to the driver talk about the challenges of making a living in the west of Ireland. 'It's not easy, but I'd rather be a taximan here than in Dublin, I'll tell ya that. We don't have the traffic and we don't have that crazy deregulation that means Dublin has more taxis than Manhattan. That's ridiculous.'

Approaching the small town of Newport, we drove over the Seven Arches Bridge and onto the main street, which evoked childhood memories of buying ice cream to eat down by the river on hot summer days. I explained where my aunt lived. 'Rosaleen? Ah, that would be Rose. I know exactly where she is,' he proclaimed. Local knowledge was clearly much more valuable than satellite navigation in these parts. He turned to me again: 'You're not Ruairí, are you?' he asked. 'Her nephew?' I was baffled. How did he know my name? Maybe it was from something on the radio, or perhaps from Rosaleen herself, but the connection didn't add up.

'That's mad! I thought it was you, alright,' he laughed. 'I remember you visiting when you were a child when you'd be up visiting Eddie, Rose and Eamonn. I remember your big mop of hair.' Now, my hair has always been a bit thick and messy, but I hadn't expected it to be a feature that a local taxi driver would recognise over 20 years later. We pulled up outside Rosaleen's, and I grabbed my rucksack to pay him. 'No need for that, Ruairí, I won't be taking any money from you. This one's on the house – it's great to see you again.' It was yet more incredible generosity, especially as I hadn't even had the chance to tell him about my trip.

'Oh, would you look who it is!' Rosaleen said with delight as she opened the door. 'Come in, come in, I'll put the kettle on.' Inside, I was immediately flooded with more fond memories and a nostalgia for simpler times in my life. For the next few hours, Rosaleen took me through family photographs, including one featuring that big head of hair the taxi driver had remembered so well. Her warmth and welcome filled my heart. It felt good to be reconnecting with the Cavan side of my family, albeit here in the west, and to hear stories about my late grandmother Maisie, with whom I had a strong connection as a child. Though I hadn't planned this stop, something in me must have known I needed it.

The next morning, I lay in bed recalling my childhood and those happy days visiting Rosaleen and her late husband, Eddie, who used to take us salmon fishing in the nearby Nephin Beg mountain range. I remembered the vastness of those mountains, Eddie's constant joking, his distinctive, gravelly laugh, and the rush of catching my first salmon. There was a purity and wildness to it all. No computer game had ever given me the same sense of wonder as that time spent with Eddie in the heights of the mountains.

At breakfast my cousin Eamonn joined us, telling me about the local carpet and flooring business he'd set up just before the economic crash. Somehow, he had stuck it out. Many of his friends hadn't been so fortunate. Some had found work in North Mayo building the controversial Corrib gas refinery – the area's only major source of employment – while others had emigrated. He described how a 'planeload' of islanders from nearby Achill Island had moved to Sweden for work and returned every seven weeks to visit wives, children and girlfriends back in Ireland. 'Emigration hurts families, decimates sports teams and leaves a big void in the community. That's the reality around these parts, as in much of the west,' he said with resignation. 'It has been that way for a long time.'

'Ah, Ruairí, you're not going so soon?' Rosaleen lamented when I announced my departure. My heart melted. I could tell how much the visit had meant to her. I had neglected to stay in touch, and I kicked myself for it. All this talk about respecting our elders, but I hadn't made much time for Rosaleen or the other older people in my life. I resolved to do better, but for now I needed to be on my way. With my eyes welling up, I hugged her goodbye and crossed the road to hitch onwards towards North Mayo.

6

Italians, Oilmen and Ancients

Mulranny to Sligo

'GOOD MAN. HITCHING, EH? I HAVEN'T SEEN ANYONE hitching in ages,' came a voice from someone walking behind me as I waited for a car to take me towards Mulranny. 'I used to hitch myself, years ago. I went all over France, slept on park benches and all over. Those were the days,' the man said before wishing me good luck and continuing on his way. *What stories he must have*, I thought. I was speculating about how this man's life might have changed when a big, shiny car pulled up, taking me by surprise. I had completely forgotten where I was for a moment, blissfully unaware I had my thumb out.

'I don't normally stop for people,' said the driver. 'In fact, it's my first time ever picking someone up.' I wasn't going to hold this against him, especially as I hadn't seen another hitchhiker so far on my entire trip. Alan Gielty owned a well-known bar and restaurant on nearby Achill Island, one of the most popular tourist hotspots in the region. Like most people I had met, he was excited about the current heatwave that was lifting the national mood, ripping into one of those 99 ice cream cones that Irish people go mad for when the sun comes out. 'You can't beat it,' he said, with a big grin. Alan's business had gone through tough times but was bouncing back after he invested heavily in renovations and renewed his focus on good food and drink. There it was again: talk of Ireland's food revolution.

Alan was also a volunteer with the Royal National Lifeboat Institution (RNLI), which gave him a unique view on life and death. He had encountered numerous drownings and near drownings over the years, and it informed his outlook. 'It puts life into perspective, I can tell you that,' he said in a quiet voice. After a couple of minutes' silence, during which he appeared lost in thought, he piped up again. 'Your other half, letting you off like this, she must be a great woman for putting up with you!'

'You're not wrong there, Alan,' I replied. 'I'm a lucky man, no doubt about it. Susan is a special woman.'

After Alan dropped me off in the village of Mulranny, I crossed over to the tree-lined N59 road towards Bangor Erris. It was good to have shade, but there was little traffic. I was hoping to pass by Ballinaboy, where Shell, Statoil and partners were building the Corrib gas refinery. Years ago, I got to know local people who were campaigning against the project, and I wanted to see what things were like now. When I was still waiting after half an hour, I started to get paranoid. Perhaps the occupants of the few cars that had passed thought I was part of the resistance to the refinery, on my way to a protest. The gas project was a divisive issue in the area and tensions ran high. Then again, so many people were against the project that, based on my paranoid logic, this could also help get me a lift.

Another half hour passed and only one car had gone by. Meanwhile, across the road, a constant stream of cars headed towards Achill. *Feck this*, I thought. *I'm going to Achill.*

———

Five minutes later, I was in the back of a rental car talking to two Italian tourists through a fog of loud music and cigarette smoke. Marco and Simona were from Rome and looked every bit the part: dark-skinned and bohemian, with an air of movie-star cool. 'Where are you going?' asked Marco as he tipped ash out the window. 'I'm not entirely sure,' I replied. It turned out they were on a driving holiday and had booked into a hostel for the night on Achill. 'Would you mind if I came with you?' I asked cheekily, relieved at the prospect of having found a place to spend the night. 'Sure. It's eh, no problem,' said Marco in broken English as we sped over the bridge towards the dramatic mountain rising from the centre of sun-cloaked Achill Island.

After a few missed turns and sheep-related delays, we finally made it to our hostel, located in an old, isolated farmhouse near the beach. We checked in and found our shared dorm room, which was not dissimilar to the one I had avoided back on Inishbofin. 'We are going to drive around before it gets dark,' said Marco, offering me the chance to come with them. I had planned to stay in and catch up on some blogs, but a trip around the island was too tempting to refuse.

Our first stop was one of Achill's most famous sights: Slievemore, also known as 'the deserted village', where the remains of up to 100 famine-era stone cottages pepper a mile-long stretch of road along the sloping terrain of Slievemore mountain.

The haunting memory of this place seemed to linger in the air, whispering to its visitors to never forget the suffering of those who died here or were forced to leave. I contemplated that dark period that has left scars not only on Ireland's landscape, but also on our collective psyche. Like most people, I had been taught at school that the famine, known in Irish as an Gorta Mór (the Great Hunger), was caused by blight that destroyed the Lumper harvest. Many Irish people relied on this type of potato as a dietary staple. Before the Great Hunger, Ireland's population was over 8 million. Over 1 million died of starvation, and an estimated 1.5 million emigrated – a combined loss of approximately one-quarter of the population. The Great Hunger left Ireland being one of the few countries in the world with a population lower today than in the nineteenth century. The trauma inflicted by this loss cut into the soul of Ireland, and I believe it can still be felt today.

Years later, I learned that there was actually a lot more food in Ireland at the time, but much of it was being exported to feed a growing

British empire. Some believed that the British government had allowed the famine to happen, while others even viewed it as part of a policy of genocide that served colonial interests. Charles Trevelyan, the British civil servant overseeing famine relief, described the famine as a 'mechanism for reducing surplus population', writing that 'the judgement of God sent the calamity to teach the Irish a lesson, that calamity must not be too much mitigated. The real evil with which we have to contend is not the physical evil of the Famine, but the moral evil of the selfish, perverse and turbulent character of the people.' These alarming comments tell us a lot about the brutality of British colonial rule in Ireland, but I had to remind myself that there was also no shortage of native Irish willing to profit off the backs of their people.

As I sat among the ghostly ruins contemplating the dark shadow of history, Marco caught my attention. 'You know, Ruairí, this famine, that was a real crisis. We in Italy and Ireland, we think we have a crisis. If you have no food and no house, or you are in a war, well, that's a real crisis. Mostly we are not in a crisis in that way.' He was right, of course. A blunt reminder that many of us live like kings and queens compared with 70 per cent of the planet's people who live on less than €10 per day. It was a good dose of perspective amid all the stories of hardship I was hearing.

The sun started to fade over Achill as we walked in silence back to the car. By now we were getting hungry, so we headed along to a local restaurant where I decided to splash out and buy my hosts a nice dinner. It felt good to pass on some of the kindness that had come my way. During our meal, Marco translated with Italian-style gestures as I asked Simona what she did for a living. With her style and grace, I expected to hear that she was a film director, a fashion designer or an artist. Marco's reply caught me on the hop. 'She is a street cleaner,' he said, looking at me as I awkwardly tried to hide my surprise. 'She gets up at 5am every morning and cleans the streets of Rome.' Stereotypes and prejudices had caught me in their trap. 'Oh, she likes it,' added Marco, easing my confusion. 'It is a well-paid job in Rome, and it suits her very well.'

I had never really thought much about this particular job, but I could see its value. 'Well, it's an important job,' I said. 'Humans can be pretty messy creatures and we often don't always value those who help keep our towns and cities clean for the rest of us to enjoy. Maybe it's because a lot of the cleaning happens late at night or early in the morning. It's like Simona is clearing the city of all the grime and negative energy, like a kind of city angel?' As Marco translated, a giant smile spread over Simona's face.

'She says yes, you are right, that's exactly how she sees it. That is her belief, and she says thank you for seeing it. She starts every day very early in the morning, before the city is awake, and she says she always puts a kind of a prayer into her work, like blessing the streets to create good energy for the millions of people who walk by each day.'

Simona's ritual reminded me of a line from Kahlil Gibran's *The Prophet*: 'Work is love made visible. And if you cannot work with love but only with distaste, it is better that you should leave your work and sit at the gate of the temple and take alms of those who work with joy.'

———

'You must come with us! We would like that,' offered Marco the next morning as I pondered my next move. The couple were heading north towards Sligo, and it seemed like I might as well go with the flow.

Things couldn't be easier. Good people, sunny weather and an easy lift. Technically this was cheating, so I walked up the road a little and stuck my thumb out for Simona and Marco to pick me up. 'Where are you going?' asked Marco. 'Sligo,' I replied. 'Oh, this is fantastic, we are going, eh, right to there,' he said, smiling.

The morning sun beat down on Achill, creating a vista that would give any Greek island a run for its money. The local sheep sweated it out in their woolly jackets as tourists made for the beaches, and locals made use of the warm weather to catch up on painting, gardening and building. We sped over the Michael Davitt Bridge, back through Mulranny and up over the vast boglands of Ballycroy National Park before hitting the Wild West outpost of Bangor. This was now oil country – or more accurately, gas country – the entry point to Ballinaboy and the region where Shell and Statoil had waged their battle to build a giant gas refinery and high-pressure pipeline on unstable bogland in one of Europe's most unspoilt regions. It was an area of fishermen and farmers, an emerging eco-tourism and adventure sports destination, and a refuge for the Irish language, culture and rebel spirit.

I'd first visited the area several years ago after hearing an Irish nun called Sr. Majella McCarron deliver a passionate presentation about the multinational oil companies' building plans. 'They will stop at nothing,' Sr Majella had exclaimed. 'They will weave their way around government, media, the clergy, whatever it takes to get the gas, and don't fool yourself about their promises of protecting health, safety and the environment. This is about cold profit, pure and simple. The rest is PR.' I remember feeling the hairs on my arms tingle and thinking: *This is serious, this is different.* I ended up meeting locals and joining their ten-year, David-versus-Goliath campaign to challenge the project.

In the end, after no small number of beatings and jailings, the project proceeded. Goliath had prevailed. The locals, supported by campaigners from around the world, had fought a brave fight, but ultimately, they could not fend off the might of corporate power. However, the protesters had scored important victories along the way. Their legal appeals and consistent pressure helped secure improvements in the pipeline and refinery process. The courage they showed and lessons they learned inspired communities worldwide in battles against fracking and other threats to the environment and public health.

'It is the same problem in many places,' Marco said, after I explained some of what had transpired. 'Corporations are now more powerful than governments. It is not good for democracy. They even own and control most of the media, meaning they can shape the news we see and don't see.' *It's depressing*, I thought, looking towards the near-completed refinery and the fading graffiti, placards and 'Shell out' signs that dotted an otherwise unspoilt landscape.

We drove on to Kilcommon. The roads were quiet, with no sign of the trucks, police or protesters that had been such a feature of recent years. To the untrained eye, there wasn't much to look at beyond the exceptional beauty of the bay, but all around were telltale signs, gates and barriers, industrial scars on the landscape and an eerie sense that the battle of Erris had come to an end. 'This situation reminds me of the story of Enrico Mattei,' Marco said, breaking the silence. 'He was a famous politician who tried to change the way Italy managed its energy supply. The powerful people did all they could to stop him – in the end, he died in a mysterious plane crash. One report suggested it was a bomb. It is worth reading about, and there is even a movie. Yes, it is well known that you do not mess with the oilmen, but you know, no matter what the obstacles, we need to keep fighting for what is right.'

———

Our sobering journey through gas country finally dropped us in Belmullet, the area's main market town. Like most small Irish towns, it has one main street, lots of pubs and small shops, and few younger people. Yet Belmullet looked busier than most towns, a stream of shoppers and cars contributing to a hive of activity. Though long-term sustainability had been overlooked in the refinery's construction, there was no doubt the extra builders, engineers, security guards and police had brought a short-term cash injection to a region that badly needed it.

We stopped for food at a local café, but any plans for a restful lunch were soon put to bed. I was pulled away by a call from journalist Brian O'Connell, who wanted to write a feature on my trip for the *Irish Times*, followed by a call from BBC Radio Foyle in Derry looking for an interview. The trip was now attracting a large following online and the media was increasingly interested in reporting on it. 'I'll tell you what,' I told the BBC researcher, 'I'll hitch up to Derry early tomorrow morning and do an interview in the studio.' The words had fallen out of my mouth. It was quite a distance to Derry, and I hadn't planned to go there. However, it seemed as good an idea as any.

After lunch, we drove down the Mullet Peninsula – another gem in Ireland's impressive crown of natural treasures that I had never visited. I looked out on fishermen mending boats on the rugged shore and children playing on pristine, empty beaches. At the end of the peninsula, we stopped at the Blacksod Lighthouse. I couldn't resist the temptation to go for a swim in the sparkling water. Swimming in the sea had offered me so much respite over the years – a natural medicine in moments when I got worked up about the state of the world. *This is bliss*, I thought as I floated on my back with the sun on my face, Marco and Simona's laughter carrying from a distance on the calm breeze.

The afternoon serenity seemed in stark contrast to the industrialisation happening not far away. In an area blighted by unemployment and centuries of emigration, I could understand why some supported the gas refinery. Yet, as I looked around at this unspoilt landscape, I imagined a world where humanity could meet its needs by working in harmony with the planet rather than constantly pushing to drill, extract and exploit. I remembered Sr. Majella's speech and the stories of Enrico Mattei and those who had sacrificed their safety, their health and even their lives for causes greater than profit. Whether or not we won every battle was not the point. There could never be any victory if we didn't stand up and fight.

———

As we drove towards Sligo, I was in my element. There was only one problem: the music. Marco and Simona had been playing the same CD all day – a compilation of famous Irish ballads sung by a cover band. As much as I loved 'The Fields of Athenry', I'd had my fill. 'Marco, I need to stop here for a minute, please,' I requested as we passed back through Belmullet. I jumped out and ran into the nearest shop filled with children's toys. 'Have you no music at all?' I pleaded with the shopkeeper. 'I'm being driven mad by a bad rendition of "The Fields of Athenry"! Surely you have something?'

'Well, no, I don't, to be honest, but let me think.' The shopkeeper hesitated. 'Give me a second. I have these CDs here.' He pulled out a wallet of CDs and handed me one by the Waterboys. 'Just give me a euro.'

Within two minutes, I was back in the car, handing over our new soundtrack and attempting to explain to the confused Italians how I got a CD for one euro in a toy shop. 'Oh, I don't really know,' I responded.

'It's Ireland. You get used to things not making sense.' On we went over the bumpy road to Ballina, Marco puffing away on his cigarette and me trying to use my laptop in the back seat while the Waterboys blasted out over the boglands of North Mayo.

I needed to make progress in order to get to Sligo and then on to Derry for the radio interview, but about half an hour before we reached Ballina I remembered a young community worker called Louise Heneghan who had said to get in touch if I was in the area. I gave her a call, and Marco and Simona agreed to stop so I could do a very quick interview with her.

'Do you mind if we find somewhere quieter to chat?' I asked Louise after she arrived into the busy service station.

'No probs,' she replied as we headed across the road, ending up on the grounds of a fire station. 'This is all a bit random,' Louise remarked, laughing.

'Absolutely,' I agreed. 'This whole trip is pretty random, but great.'

Louise was 23, had recently finished a social care degree, and was back living at home and working part-time in respite care while trying to find other work opportunities. 'I want to inspire students to follow their dreams,' she told me when I asked about her plan to qualify as a teacher. 'Lack of employment here is the main challenge. Most of the young people I know around here are completely disillusioned. I love the west of Ireland, but there is nothing for young people here. Ballina has a huge issue with youth mental health and suicide, which is partially caused by the lack of opportunities.'

I asked Louise what she hoped would change in Ireland. 'If there was political reform, we'd gain trust in politicians,' she replied. 'I keep hopeful because, eventually, we'll see a different country. Possibly 10 or 20 years down the road.' I left Louise feeling inspired. Here in rural County Mayo was a young woman resisting the temptation to emigrate or move to the city, determined to stay and fight for her community. It wasn't easy, but her passion was evident; I had no doubt she was someone who would make a mark.

We set off once again for Sligo, driving along the N59 between stone walls that flanked a sunny sea of green fields. 'So, what are your thoughts about Ireland so far?' I put to Marco and Simone, interested in his outside perspective.

'It is wonderful,' Marco said. 'We love it. There is a lot of litter, we see. The drinking is a problem, and the radio doesn't have good music, but the land, the people, they are incredible. It is a great country,' he concluded, summing up so much in so few words. Of course, I would have preferred that they hadn't spotted our shortcomings, but it was clear that Ireland had charmed them. The sunny weather no doubt helped, as did the romance that flowed between these two Roman lovers, but beyond that, Ireland had cast its spell on them, as it does so many. Observing this in visitors is always therapeutic, a reminder that, for all its flaws, Ireland remains a very special island with lots to celebrate.

As we neared Sligo, the hill of Knocknarea rose in the distance, revealing the outline of Queen Méabh's grave on its peak. According to legend, the warrior Queen Méabh of Connacht once reigned supreme in this region, and was a powerful goddess figure whom kings and chieftains would symbolically marry during their inauguration rituals. It is also said she was the inspiration for the fairy Queen Mab found in William Shakespeare's *Romeo and Juliet*. Whoever she was, she certainly left her mark on these parts with her grave high atop Knocknarea – an imposing landmark. This was also an area where William Butler Yeats spent much of his time, no doubt inspired by the myth, legend and natural beauty that make Sligo such an enchanting place.

We turned off the main road, passing along tree-cloaked country roads before reaching the foot of Knocknarea, climbing it to look out on the surfers of Strandhill Beach and the Bluestack Mountains across the waters of Donegal Bay. Knocknarea, translated from the Irish Cnoc na Riogha, is said to mean "hill of the kings", and this was a view fit for a king – or a queen, for that matter.

We drove the short distance to the renowned megalithic tombs of Carrowmore. It was evening and the visitor centre was closed, so we hopped over the fence and into the fields. About 30 giant boulder monuments stood, imposing and mysterious, eerily lit by the pinkish evening light that descended around us. Marco and Simona stood in awe of the massive stone structures that appeared to stare at us, daring us to understand their origins. 'What is this place?' asked Marco, intrigued.

'It's an ancient burial complex, one of the largest in Europe, dating back over 5,000 years or more, older than the pyramids of Egypt,' I replied, trying my best to do justice to this truly incredible site.

The sun ebbed as farmers worked their tractors in adjacent fields of hay. A warm evening breeze washed over us as we stood, absorbing this place's strange, serene and ancient aura. Several rabbits scurried about, and a horse approached the fence separating the grave site from a neighbouring lot, luring Simona over to stroke its mane. Marco followed, they smiled, kissed and hugged, illuminated by the soft glow of the setting sun. Time seemed to stand still.

———

'It has been a fantastic time,' said Marco, as he and Simona dropped me in Sligo. Our journey together had come to an end. Simona spoke something in Italian to Marco, then unclasped her necklace and handed it to me. 'It is her special charm for you to wear for your trip, for good luck,' Marco explained. It had only been 24 hours since I had met them, but it seemed like forever. I felt a connection outside of language and culture that comes with sharing special moments, a trust that comes with openness to adventure. I didn't know if I'd ever see them again, but I would forever remember our short time together exploring this little piece of paradise.

In Sligo, I arranged a quick catch-up with my old friend, Rodney Lancashire. Rodney, originally from Cavan, was a bit of a hero for my friends and I when we were young. He was in a thrash metal band called Richard III that became well known around Ireland. He was also from a Protestant family, which made him a minority in our mostly Catholic town.

Rodney had long since replaced his electric guitar with a concertina and banjo and had become one of the most respected traditional Irish musicians in the region. I asked Rodney his thoughts on the state of the nation. 'Oh, that could take the rest of your evening,' he said, smiling.

'We don't seem to have anyone that really wants to support the country. They're all involved with wanting to lick the arse of these multinationals, big countries, and everything like that. We don't have anyone saying, "Let's do our own thing and not be so caught up with this kind of one-world government situation." For example, down in Erris with the gas, why didn't the country secure that for ourselves, hire the expertise in, get away from the oil?'

Rodney expressed a kind of euro-scepticism that I had come across elsewhere in rural Ireland, but wasn't often reported. 'I don't think the euro really works for this country,' he said. 'Our main trading partner is the UK. At least when we had the punt, we could adjust it. We need to become more self-sufficient, not be as reliant on imports. You'd like to see that kids don't have to emigrate and that our resources aren't just given away to multinationals who make the real profit. Still,' he continued, 'you can give out about everything, but we're standing here and it's a beautiful day. For me, I just try to enjoy what I have, keep playing the music and remember that life is short. Very short.'

Like the farmer I had met in Connemara, Rodney seemed to find hope in music beyond all else. 'There are ten-year-olds that play like 70-year-olds. People from all over the world are playing Irish music now. People are coming here to learn. The music, the tradition, it's part of everything, especially here in the west of Ireland – tunes named after players and places. It's probably the main thing that has stayed in Ireland all these years. A lot of it is memorised, meaning it can never be taken from us.

'So, are you sticking around for a few tunes tonight?' Rodney asked. His invitation was tempting, but I knew it had the potential to set me off course. It was getting late, and I needed to get to Derry. Before I could head north, I had something else to attend to. A Sligo-based photographer, James Connolly, had been in touch. He wanted my photograph to accompany Brian O'Connell's article for the *Irish Times*, and I had agreed to meet him before I left town.

By the time James arrived, the light was fading quickly. Saying goodbye to Rodney, I felt a tinge of embarrassment. Being whisked off to have my photo taken for the paper – that seemed more like showbiz than the humble hitching mission I had intended. 'We need to get moving before it gets dark,' said James as we headed off through Sligo's narrow streets in his car, out past Tobernalt Holy Well and Lough Gill and up a series of hilly roads until we were looking right over County Sligo.

'I thought it was best if we'd catch a photo of you hitching, and the backdrop here is amazing,' said James, indicating that he wanted me to pose for a shot. It was all very cringe-worthy. At least nobody would see me doing it up here in the hills. I also wasn't going to argue with James Connolly, a man with the same name as one of Ireland's most famous revolutionaries. 'You stand there, face this way and put your thumb out,' commanded James as I followed his orders to move my thumb in and out, my shoulder this way and that, until I had struck the perfect hitching pose, complete with an idyllic backdrop.

'Fake hitchhiking for a newspaper photo shoot. James, this is pretty ridiculous. How on earth did I end up doing this?'

James shrugged and laughed. 'I don't know, Ruairí. You tell me!'

7

The Way Forward
Is the Way Back

Bundoran to Mountcharles

BUNDORAN, OR 'FUNDORAN' AS IT'S SOMETIMES JOKINGLY called thanks to its seaside attractions, holds a special place in my heart. My mother grew up on its main street in her parents' bed and breakfast, known as St Patrick's House. My grandmother Mary Malone moved there from Killimor, in rural east County Galway, in the early 1950s to join my grandfather Dan Keenaghan. They raised six children, hosting tourists, running a small shop and a small farm, working in the bog, and doing whatever work they could find when the cold winds of winter left the town feeling empty. I visited them every Christmas and summer, observing how they lived as good, hard-working people loyal to family, Church, State, and the Fianna Fáil party.

In my early twenties, I was living in Canada when I was offered a short-term research contract in nearby Ballyshannon. I jumped at the chance, which not only allowed me to travel all over the beautiful northwest but also to spend six months living with my elderly grand-parents. It was an incredibly special time, sitting on dark winter nights listening to their stories and reflections on how the world had changed since their youth in the 1930s and 1940s.

It was the winter of 2002, and the country was booming. Every second conversation was about property, investing, holidays and how we had it made. However, cracks were starting to appear. People's lives seemed to be growing busier and more stressful, and revelations about abuses of power by both Church and State started to emerge.

Every evening at 6pm I'd join my grandparents in their living room and watch the Angelus, a 60-second call to prayer broadcast daily on Irish public television. They would sit or kneel and recite their prayers, while I joined in spirit, not knowing the actual words. The news would immediately follow, bulletins inevitably focused on our 'miracle' economy, followed by the weather forecast, which is compulsory watching in many Irish households.

When news of Church child-abuse scandals and cover-ups appeared on television, tension would descend upon the room. I wanted to shout with rage about young children being abused by those who claimed to be God's representatives. Looking at them as they watched the news in silence, I realised that in many ways my grandparents' world was collapsing around them.

When it came to politics, there was also some tension. My grandfather was dismayed by the trend towards development that he said 'favoured the big man against the little man.'

Meanwhile, the fog of war was descending. The horrific attacks on New York and Washington on 11 September 2001 provided the necessary cover for US president George W. Bush to invade Iraq, cheered on by the oil industry. I started organising meetings, protests and vigils to oppose what was widely viewed as a deceptive, illegal and immoral war. I wrote to the local papers and started speaking on the radio, cutting my teeth as a campaigner while learning how to harness the power of media and the internet.

I sent a registered letter to Nelson Mandela when I learned he was coming to Ireland, hoping it would arrive before his address at the university in Galway. In it I urged him to encourage Ireland's leaders to oppose the war and to stop providing refuelling facilities to the US military at Shannon Airport. Although Mandela didn't refer directly to Shannon Airport in his speech, his message to Ireland was clear. He said any country that sidelined the UN was a 'danger to the world' and that 'they do so because you are keeping quiet. You are afraid of this country and its leader. You say that if you take an independent stand, you will not be able to get support from it.' As I watched the livestream of Mandela's speech, I knew it was impossible to know if he had read my letter, but his speech struck a chord. It was a reminder at an important time in my life to never be afraid to speak out.

My grandfather worried about my activism. Like many of his generation, he grew up with a relatively narrow and positive view of the US, a country that had provided refuge for millions of Irish people, including members of my grandparents' families. The US was seen as a beacon of hope and freedom, to which Ireland was indebted. To question it was simply wrong.

I understood my grandfather's perspective and had shared his admiration for the United States and its people. I had spent several months working there on various trips, and always came away grateful for the warm welcomes I received and inspired by the people I met. Many of these people were proud Americans, but not shy about challenging their government when necessary. Eventually, however, it dawned on me that my grandfather wasn't worried simply because we disagreed about foreign policy. At the heart of it was his concern that I might land myself in trouble by sticking my neck above the parapet.

My grandparents grew up in a relatively authoritarian state, a fragile post-independence Ireland carrying the wounds of war, poverty and emigration. In the not-too-distant past, across the border minutes from where my grandparents lived, people had been shot, killed and disappeared for speaking out. The lesson from hundreds of years of Irish history was that dissent is risky and can result in danger or isolation.

While living with my grandparents, I started to think about what I really wanted to do with my life. After joining my grandparents in their nightly prayers, I'd work late into the night drawing up lists, plans and dreams of how to change the world. I was 25 and my job, researching young people's mental health, was about to end. Although the funding had dried up, I started to wonder if this subject was something I could continue to pursue as part of a wider social mission. I was tired of merely opposing things. I wanted to build something.

Now, here I was all these years later in 2014, sleeping in that same old bed at my 89-year-old grandmother's house, reconnecting with that time in my life when I was bursting with ideas, energy and passion.

'We used to wonder what you were up to in that room,' Gran told me as we sat sharing fond memories. 'You were always writing things down, making plans, buzzing around the place. Dan would be proud to see you now.' My grandfather was no longer with us, having passed away six years previously after a brave battle with cancer, but it felt like his spirit was with us that night, listening in and smiling as my gran and I reminisced about that special time together.

It was getting late, but I wanted to hear more from my gran about what life was like long ago. 'People were happy because they had more of a social life, you see. You had to get on with your neighbour, and he needed you. Now you don't have to. Now there's the phone and all that.

'Everybody knew each other. If you went out on the road they'd be walking and cycling. Now you see them whizzing by. There was a lot more poverty, too, but still people helped each other. You might have a bit more and share, and others would share with you when they had more.'

I knew my grandmother's life hadn't always been easy, but she pointed to a link between simplicity and happiness that was emerging as a strong theme on my trip.

'We'll say a prayer now,' she said as bedtime arrived.

'We will, indeed,' I replied, knowing I wouldn't get to share many more moments like this with her. I took to my knees and looked to the seat where Dan used to sit. With a nod and a smile, I offered thanks for my grandparents and the love they'd given me over the years.

———

In the morning, my uncle Daniel arrived to drive me to the outskirts of Ballyshannon. I was particularly fond of his gentle manner and wisdom. Daniel and his family had been through a lot, including a relentless battle to get decent services for his son Christopher, who was born with cerebral palsy. Daniel faced huge challenges but had found a way through and was developing a Zen-like calm that prompted me to nickname him Morrie, after the wise old man in Mitch Albom's book *Tuesdays with Morrie*.

When he dropped me off, I asked Daniel if he had any words of advice to offer.

'The main thing is to keep it simple. I've found that if you don't get enough rest, it's very difficult to cope with life. Sometimes people expect too much of themselves, but don't be afraid to dream. It is dreams that create the future, and sometimes as we get older, we look back and think, why did I not believe in myself more?' With those parting words, Daniel smiled and waved me on my way.

Here it was again, something I obviously needed to hear: simplicity. As my trip's momentum continued to build, it was getting more complicated than I originally envisaged. I was hitching and talking to people during the day, doing media interviews, and staying up until 2am writing blogs and replying to messages. I was waking up in a different bed each morning, and although I was hardly roughing it, I was starting to tire. Daniel's advice was timely.

PJ the fishmonger picked me up on the road to Donegal. 'Ah yes, indeed, of course I know who your grandparents are. Ah, poor Dan is no longer with us. He was a great man.' As it happened, PJ used to park his white van across the street from my grandparents' house in Bundoran once a week and sell fresh fish he had collected straight from the boats in Killybegs that morning. Fresh fish didn't always penetrate the landlocked confines of Cootehill when I was growing up, and I had fond memories of going to see 'the fish man'.

'I was always happy with keeping my business small and avoiding all the stress of growing bigger,' he told me. 'There was an old boy named Sonny who used to come visit me. He used to say, "PJ, you're better with a small fire that'll keep ya warm than a big fire that'll burn ya." I saw others expand during the boom, and they often took on too much and are paying the price now. By keeping it small, I've managed to stay free from a lot of those problems.'

He dropped me off on the Letterkenny Road, just outside Donegal Town, where I suddenly remembered I had a radio interview. As the phone rang, I jumped over a fence into a field to get away from the traffic noise. I crouched beneath a hedge as my interview started and looked up to find myself staring directly into the eyes of a sheep. Here I was in Donegal, in a sheep-filled field surrounded by dung and sheep noises while doing a live radio interview. I couldn't help but laugh.

———

Around me, the mountains of Donegal flickered with golden sparkles that rippled into the nearby sea. I didn't fancy jumping into another car so soon, so I decided to sit and think about my next move. I had already messaged the BBC to tell them I probably wouldn't make it to Derry in time for our interview, and they kindly agreed to do it by phone. So, I was in no rush. I decided to call my good friend Keith who happened to live nearby in the hope that he was around.

'Ah yeah, Ruairí, I'm just on my way to St. John's Point to map out a walking route and then go for a swim, if you fancy it,' he replied over the phone. 'I'll pick you up in ten minutes.'

I had met Keith ten years previously at a peace rally I helped organise at the start of the Iraq war, where he read a poem he had written called 'From Darkness to Light'. Weeks later, we organised another event marking George W. Bush's visit to Dromoland Castle near Shannon Airport, where he was welcomed by the Irish government, led by Bertie Ahern. We had wanted to go and protest but decided to keep it local and created an event called Make Hay, Not War in the centre of Donegal Town.

We placed several bales of hay on the street. Keith was dressed as a farmer with pitchfork in hand and proceeded to chase me – in a suit and Bush mask – shouting, 'Wait till I get ya, you're in for it, Bush.' It was quite the scene, especially for afternoon shoppers. At one stage, a tour bus full of Americans parked beside us and we had a chance to chat to them about the war. Our event made the front page of the local paper, meaning our message reached many more thousands than it might have if we had gone to Dromoland Castle.

After that, I collaborated with Keith on several projects. We worked well together, and this prompted me in 2004 to ask if he'd join in establishing the Community Creations organisation, which later gave birth to SpunOut.ie.

Initially, we both worked from home, each relying on ridiculously slow dial-up internet connections. I was based in a small cottage near Kinlough, County Leitrim, and Keith worked from his cottage half an hour north in Laghey, County Donegal. We jokingly referred to our start-up as a cottage industry.

We were soon joined by Anna Lally, a talented Donegal journalist who helped to spearhead the development of SpunOut.ie. It was tough at the start, and we had little income, but there was a real wind behind us. We undertook all sorts of consultancy, campaigning and publishing projects until eventually we had enough money to rent a historic three-storey house in Ballyshannon, which we nicknamed The Beehive and turned into a hub for all sorts of community activities.

The house was imbued with a sense of history and mystery, aided by the fact the famous poet William Allingham, best known for his poem 'The Faeries', was born there in 1824. Ballyshannon, a small, hilly border town on the River Erne, had been through its fair share of troubles. Said to be Ireland's oldest town, the Vikings, Gaelic chieftain Red Hugh O'Donnell and the British all used it as a strategic gateway. The ruins of an old famine workhouse, where the destitute sought shelter as a last-ditch attempt to stay alive, offered a chilling reminder that the town had also suffered greatly during the Great Hunger.

I always felt it was a special place for us to have started an organisation together, often reflecting on this during lunchtime walks to a plaque at the River Erne that mentions how the river is also known as the River of the Morning Star. I knew that in some cultures the Morning Star, another name for Venus, represents hope in the world as it shines bright in the morning sky, ending the darkness of night as it ushers in the dawn. It was powerful symbolism.

Now here Keith and I were, years later, having taken different paths but still good friends. 'Those were mad days, Ruairí, weren't they?'

Keith said as we set off towards the sea. 'It's great what you are doing with this trip because that is what people have been doing for generations, going out seeking answers,' he told me. 'It's so important because we find ourselves at a crossroads, not only in Ireland but because we're so connected now, globally and into Europe. What we're feeling now is a hangover from something that began in maybe the 1950s and 1960s, and that's consumerism and profit-driven growth and individualism.' It lifted quality of life, he said, allowing for better homes, travel and sexual freedom. However, 'we're faced now with the downside, a country where community has been neglected. You hear Ireland called Ireland Inc., like the whole country is a corporate identity. I see it in my own community. It wreaks havoc on people. People feel disempowered.'

Years ago, people were more self-reliant, possessing the skills to build their own houses, fix their own cars, grow their own food. Today, Keith said, people's prosperity seems predicated on the whims of the market. 'We have less and less chance to be kind, to help each other. There's a great sense of wellbeing from kindness.'

On the other hand, Keith warned against looking back with too much nostalgia. 'A man I met from Longford talked about the number of men and women in his rural area that never got married. These people didn't have much of an opportunity to better themselves. Often, they were very intelligent. It was tragic. They weren't allowed to get married because maybe the eldest son had got the farm and maybe the daughter didn't have any wealth to bring with her into marriage. This was awful, and it was happening in Ireland until the mid-twentieth century.'

Yes, people then had closer connections to the land through farming and the bog, Keith pointed out, but often these positive aspects of country life were accompanied by poverty and repression.

I asked Keith how these thoughts around community manifested in his own life.

'We're starting to grow bits and pieces locally. We planted 100 trees recently and we had a traditional céilí dance where young and old came together and had a great night. I also think random acts of kindness are important. I do a lot of writing and cover local events that are happening. The amount of goodwill I receive in response is huge. When you break the isolation and do things for other people, you feel a lot better. We are social beings, and we need to rethink and reimagine society. We don't have to go back to living in caves. We can keep the wealth that we have, harness technology, and create a vibrant, healthy, social, caring society.'

Keith's words made perfect sense as we travelled up remote roads on the narrow peninsula leading to St. John's Point. As the car climbed, Donegal Bay appeared in our view, the sparkling sea reflecting the sun's beams – a world away from the wild Atlantic rain and wind that often dominates in these parts.

Sometime later we arrived at the serene-looking Coral Beach, where the only people around were some local men repairing a boat, and a family with two kids who were busy building sand castles and enjoying what might as well have been a private beach.

The sea called us to cool off in its gentle waves. We stripped to our boxer shorts and jumped in with blissful abandon. 'I never thought I'd be so thankful for the cold Atlantic water,' Keith said as we swam in this secluded oasis.

Back at the car, I noticed the time and started to panic. 'Shit, shit . . . I was supposed to be on the radio a few minutes ago,' I said, noticing a missed call on my phone. I clicked to reply, apologised, and within 60 seconds was on air. 'So here he is, the hitchhiker who is on his way to Derry,' the presenter announced in a friendly northern accent.

I sat in the passenger seat and talked away about my motivations and experiences. It was going well, except for the fact I was dripping wet. Sitting in my soggy boxer shorts, I was glad the listeners couldn't see me. Between hanging out with sheep live on air a couple of hours ago, and talking to the BBC in wet underwear, it seemed I was also innovating in the world of live radio.

———

On the way back to Donegal Town, Keith and I stopped to see our mutual friend Larry Masterson. Larry had recently retired as a regional manager after 35 years with the health service. He had been hugely supportive of Keith and I in the early days. He was one of those important outsiders on the inside, a former social worker frustrated by State bureaucracy who done his best to initiate and support grassroots work from within the system.

Since his retirement, Larry had been following his dream of setting up a social farm on land he owned in Mountcharles, just outside Donegal Town.

'Welcome to Blissberry Farm,' a radiant-looking Larry shouted as he bounced over to us with a beaming smile. 'This is where it all happens, lads. Come on over, I have a picnic made up for us to enjoy.'

This was a treat: a feast of fresh produce from Larry's farm, in the company of good people.

'Things are moving. The farm is getting busier and busier. The whole idea of social farming is to bring people back to the land, especially people who have been through hard times, and to help them reconnect with themselves, with others and with the earth.

'I had one young lad here recently who had been written off by the doctor. He was with the doctor for five minutes before being sent home with a diagnosis of depression and a prescription for medication. He was lying around the house. His friends were unemployed, emigrating, drinking and generally losing interest in life. I talked to his parents and got him down here and gave him seeds to plant some vegetables.

'Before long he was down tending to his vegetables, which he ended up selling at a market. It might seem simple, but the experience awoke something in him, gave him a purpose and got him excited about life. I'm not saying that doctors and medication don't have a role to play. They can be lifesavers for people. Ideally, we'd all work together, but there's no doubt we need to move away from a medical model that is too reliant on pharmaceutical interventions and not placing enough value on talking, sharing, listening and learning.

'When you bring someone down here and their confidence is low and you introduce them to animals like these horses, you give them a brush and they start to see the effects on that animal – I'd argue money or drugs won't have the same effect.' Caring for animals can teach self-respect and more, Larry said. 'We've a young woman at the moment fighting cancer. It lifts her out of bed in the morning to come down here and groom the ponies. I didn't look for that. She asked me if she could do it.

'I've also seen it firsthand in Italy, at a social farm there, where people with dementia visit a local farm for a few hours each day. When they return to their care home, they feel better and sleep better. It's not rocket science; the fresh air, a bit of exercise, the human interaction – it's all part of a healthy society, and it's time the health services moved in this direction. Besides, it'll actually save the State money.'

All around us was sea, mountains, green fields and fresh, healthy food. Larry looked happier than I'd ever seen him. It was easy to see how people would receive healing in a place like this.

'Fair play to him,' said Keith after we said goodbye to Larry and continued on our way.

'The system is stripping away the beauty of life. It's no wonder there's a mental health crisis. What he is doing is the future. What I love about it is that it's a modern way based on the traditions of people helping each other. It's the way forward. Funny, in some ways, the way forward is the way back.'

———

'Do you remember that day on the bog with your grandfather?' Keith asked as we ventured back towards Donegal. 'How could I forget?' I replied, recalling a particular afternoon on Keith's small patch of bog several years ago.

My grandfather Dan was always talking about the bog. The bog this, the bog that. 'We used to go for the day and work so far, but the chat was powerful, and people would be singing away together. When lunchtime came, we'd have tea and sandwiches and it would taste amazing. Nothing beats the fresh air in a bog. It could heal anything. If you ever had any troubles in your life, the bog could help you,' he told me one night as he sat in his chair, an ageing king in his castle.

I recalled a day when Keith phoned to say he was on his way to the bog to collect fuel for the fires of the long Donegal winter nights. I decided to bring my grandfather up, to get him out of the house and away from the negative news that was agitating him in his final years.

'Ah, good man, Keith, you're hard at it,' he said as he arrived, wearing a sun hat and the look of an old sage on a pilgrimage to the disappearing world of his youth.

'Just in time, Dan. I could do with some expert help around here,' said Keith, picking up on the significance of the moment. My grandfather was in his late seventies, but vestiges of his once fierce physical strength were still evident as he proceeded to give us a master class in how to properly cut and stack the turf.

For the next couple of hours, he regaled us with tales of suffering and salvation in those bogs where once great forests grew. There were tears in his eyes when it came time to leave. Like most Irish men of his generation, he did his best to hide emotion. Keith and I respected his moment, but the depth of the experience was evident.

It was fitting that a photo of Dan in the bog from that day took pride of place on the altar at his funeral. After all, it was to be his last time in the bog, an experience he'd talk about until his final days.

8

The Hero's Journey

Letterkenny to Derry

THEY SAY THE TEACHER APPEARS WHEN THE STUDENT is ready, and I was prepared for Tim, who announced his arrival in a blaze of glory. I had been hitching on the road to Letterkenny no more than three minutes when a small red car almost swayed off the road to offer me a lift.

'Ah, you're on a Hero's Journey,' said Tim, a sociology lecturer and former priest who was on his way to a recovery meeting in Letterkenny. 'The hitching – it's obvious you heard the call to adventure and answered it. That's how you go about finding the gold,' he said, comparing my trip to the Hero's Journey, a template developed by mythologist Joseph Campbell.

Campbell proposed that most of the world's cultures and religions have a common myth, reflected in everything from the heroes of Irish legend to Greek mythology. It's a tale that has been told a thousand times, more recently in *Star Wars*, *Harry Potter*, *Lord of the Rings*, *The Hunger Games* and beyond. It is the story of an individual called or pushed into an adventure, often reluctantly, who then finds the courage to proceed while facing down foes and being helped by allies. Eventually, the hero conquers some kind of dragon and returns home with gold – or wisdom. I wasn't sure how well my trip fitted with the Hero's Journey, though I could certainly say I had felt the call to action. Furthermore, I was meeting heroes all around me – people like Tim who demonstrated tremendous resilience and strove to live life to the fullest.

Tim went on to describe his years as a priest, his challenges around addiction, and his thoughts on living a good life. 'We're all here for a reason, to find a true calling that life is calling us to. We're better able to serve others when we're fulfilling our own meaning at the same time.'

I asked him what this meant for his own life.

'I could be sitting in a university teaching back in the United States, but I chose not to because I wasn't happy, and I felt I wasn't true to myself. I have found, in my spiritual journey, that if I don't look into myself and answer my own questions, then I'm in no place to be of service to others.

'We all have within us this desire to be a success and to achieve our best in life. But, of course, it's not just a physical best, it's also a spiritual best. We are meant for something great. In my own recovery from alcoholism, I see it like that quote from the Psalms: "Come to me, all who thirst." When I was drinking, I was trying to fulfil something that could never be fulfilled with alcohol. I think it's a desire for something deeper that we often only get later in life. There's a book out now by a man with the name of Richard Rohr – *Immortal Diamond*. He's talking about that part of us within, the divine part of us that can only be fulfilled through getting to know our spiritual selves.'

———

Tim dropped me at the Mount Errigal Hotel, where I had arranged to meet my old friend Janet Gaynor. Janet had been an important mentor in my early twenties, and it felt fitting to be meeting in Letterkenny, where we'd first met. At the time, I had recently returned to my parents' house in Cootehill after being away for over a year and a half in Australia and New Zealand. I had been offered a job as a recruitment consultant but couldn't bring myself to take it up. By then, I was determined to dedicate myself fully to creating change in the world. I didn't know what that might look like, but I had a raw determination and an unwavering belief that it could happen.

Soon afterwards, opportunity knocked and I was offered a two-week data-entry contract with what was then the North Western Health Board in Donegal. A year later I was still there, under the mentorship of Janet and her colleagues, learning the ropes of youth work, health promotion and community development.

'It's infuriating and shows just how far we have to go,' Janet said when we sat down to talk over a meal in the hotel. She was referring to what had been dubbed the 'Lapgate incident,' when politicians debating contentious abortion legislation were found to have been boozing in the bar at Dáil Éireann, our national parliament. Later the same night one of them grabbed a female colleague and pulled her onto his lap. It had stoked controversy over the culture of misogyny and alcohol use in politics.

'That legislation is about defining a different kind of Ireland, about different possibilities, about saying something about the place of women and redefining the relationship between the Church and State,' Janet told me. 'I've been amazed at the audacity of the Catholic Church on this, and I'm not sure where their moral righteousness has come from, given everything around abuses and so on. They've been quite corrosive in terms of trying to push a point of view that is mixing up State and Church. I'm glad to be part of the change where we now begin to see another link in this chain being cut.'

The legislation in question did not give full access to abortion; it did, however, help pave the way for a national referendum on abortion, which passed in 2018. This particular legislation focused primarily on women whose lives were at risk during pregnancy, including through suicide.

'It is an important milestone in the wider campaign for women's rights,' Janet said. 'I think it's about redefining values and the kind of life we want for ourselves, less dictated by the Church. I grew up in an Ireland where the Church was very powerful. Men and women were physically separated in the church, women had to keep their heads covered in the church, and contraception wasn't even something that was talked about. The attitude surrounding sex and sexuality was wrong, where my mother had to be 'churched' after she had a child,' Janet said, referring to the practice whereby women were ceremonially blessed after childbirth to be brought back into a state of grace, under the judgment that sex was somehow sinful.

'The church that I grew up in was a church where women were second-class citizens. It was a church that promoted inequalities between women and men, rich and poor,' Janet continued. 'I did, however, experience the other side of that, through my education with the Presentation Sisters, nuns who were outside the normal sphere of influence. Many of them had worked abroad in India and elsewhere. They specifically told us, "girls, you can be anything you want to be." We weren't hearing that message anywhere else. They were mighty women.'

Returning to the contemporary situation, she explained, 'There's a redefining of who and what we are, and we won't be able to keep blaming institutions. We have to wake up and accept responsibility for ourselves. I don't think that's a bad thing.

'In the last election, I thought I was voting less for bankers and property developers. There is something about getting back to the basics, finding out what we need, getting a sense of ourselves and redefining the things that make us happy; about us being willing to watch out for each other, rather than remaining detached.'

After a long catch-up we drove over to Janet's cousin's Anne's house where we joined Anne, her husband, John, their teenage daughter Sinéad and their friend Kate. There, the discussion continued long into the night.

'The fact that the Lapgate incident occurred on a night that women's health was finally on the agenda is hugely symbolic. It is just another indicator of how far we have to go in terms of respect for women,' Kate said without hiding her frustration.

She was right. The spin doctors dismissed it as an inappropriate but forgettable incident, but there was more to it. On the night in question the bar had been particularly busy, suggesting that elected representatives somehow felt it was okay to be drinking on the night they were debating one of the most important issues of our time.

In a parliament, where only 15 per cent of elected representatives at the time were women, this painted a picture of a men's club lacking in empathy, understanding or common decency. The incident and subsequent response showed little respect for the more than 150,000 Irish women who had travelled to the UK for abortions. Nor did it suggest much respect for the memory of Savita Halappanavar, whose tragic death had forced the Protection of Life During Pregnancy legislation onto the table. The year before, Savita, a 31-year-old Indian-born dentist living in Galway, had died in hospital from a septic miscarriage after being refused an abortion on the grounds that it was illegal.

'It's unbelievable what women in this country have to put up with,' Janet remarked as we contemplated in silence.

'I think all that about women is very true,' John said after a while. 'And we have to keep in mind that men aren't immune from suffering, either. There's a lot going on for men that isn't often discussed.'

John, who had worked in finance for many years, helped set up a group that brought men of different backgrounds together to discuss the various life challenges they faced. 'There's huge stress out there among fellas,' he continued. 'You only have to look at the statistics around unemployment, depression, substance abuse and suicide. Men are crying out for support. I see it every day. That's part of the reason we started this group. A lot of it is about creating a place where people have the courage to be vulnerable.'

Confidentiality was one of the most important ground rules, John said. The collective support had been helpful to him during a difficult time and rewarding to all participants. 'When the group became empowered, it could tackle any issue. It's not that hard to go there once it becomes the norm.'

I could see why this concept of providing men with their own space for peer support was important. I had attended men's group meetings in Dublin when I was going through a particularly hard time. It was clear that many men in the group who were dealing with major challenges such as debt, divorce and depression benefited from the interaction with others who could intimately understand their positions.

Men, women, gender roles and equality – these complex issues weren't going to be solved by our discussion. But at least now, in the outrage that followed Savita Halappanavar's death, Lapgate and more, men and women were increasingly exploring their perspectives together, rather than regarding these discussions as part of a battle of the sexes.

Sinéad had been quiet most of the evening. She was in her final year of school and told me her friends were already talking about the prospect of emigration. 'I love Ireland, and I hope I don't have to leave,' she said, as we all bowed our heads and wondered whether she'd be one of the rare ones among the children from Donegal who found a way to stay in their native land.

'I'll tell you what, Ruairí,' said Anne as the night drew to an end. 'I don't know what the answers are to all these problems, but if you find out on your hitching travels, will you let us know? Who knows, maybe hitching is the way forward for all of us!' she said with a smile.

———

'What the hell is going on?' I mumbled as I awoke to knocking on my bedroom door. It was 7am, and Janet was waking me at the time we had agreed. But I had only got to sleep at 3am after staying up to write some blog updates.

It took me a few minutes to figure out where I was and what my plan was. All I wanted was a day in bed, but it was time to cross the border, and Derry City was calling.

Within minutes after Janet dropped me off on the side of the road, I was picked up by Nora and Richard.

'A trip about hope? Fair play to ya,' said Richard, a soft-spoken man with kind eyes. 'I'll tell ya a short story about hope. A few years ago, my marriage broke down. I wasn't in a good place. I was preparing to emigrate, but before I did, I went to Derry to visit a friend and say goodbye. We were out one night when I met Nora, and here I am years later, happier than ever with this wonderful woman beside me. Life is funny like that – hope can be right around the corner.'

By 9am we had whizzed past the spectacular sixth-century Grianán of Aileach fort and were well over the border. Northern Ireland's closer integration with the European Union, combined with demilitarisation as part of the 1990s peace process, meant that there were few official border markers. It felt strange that a somewhat invisible line, a human-made border now over 90 years old, had led to so much suffering. Continuing on into the outskirts of Derry City, I considered how borders acted as barriers as much as physical ones; arbitrary lines of division drawn up to defend, protect, control and ultimately separate.

However, Derry wasn't a place where the contrast between north and south was most evident, particularly as the vast majority of residents tended to identify as Irish rather than British. Yet this former heartland of the Irish Republican Army (IRA) – the Republican paramilitary organisation that sought to end British rule in Ireland – would be a good place to consider the conflict that had raged between Britain and Ireland for centuries.

The walled city of Derry, known as Londonderry to the British, is a place steeped in history. Historical references state that St. Columba founded a monastery there in the sixth century, and since the 1600s the north's second largest city has been in the thick of the push and pull over British rule in Ireland.

Nora and Richard dropped me in the city centre amid the bustle of people going to work, shop shutters opening and a new day beginning. I planned to spend the day wandering the streets, but first I'd have to store my heavy rucksack.

When I spoke with the BBC the previous day, the presenter had said to give them a shout if I needed anything when I was in Derry. It may have been a polite courtesy invite, but I decided to take them up on the offer.

I soon found myself in the waiting room of the BBC studios, looking scruffy and out of place among the journalists and office workers.

'Good man, Ruairí, good to meet ya,' said one of the staff at the station. 'Have a seat and let me get you a coffee. Absolutely no problems storing your bag! Now, are you hungry at all? Do you need to use the internet?'

The welcome couldn't have been warmer as more and more people came over to introduce themselves. Before long I was munching on fresh scones, surfing the web and chatting away to the staff as if I was a member of the team.

'Thanks for all your help, folks. I really appreciate it. I'd better head into town. I can't stop here all day,' I said.

'What are you doing in town?' the presenter wanted to know. I explained that I was looking to do vox pop audio interviews with people about life in Derry, to explore the theme of hope and the city itself.

'I'll tell you what. If you bring back some of the interviews, we'll broadcast them on our show. How does that sound?' This was a dream, a golden opportunity. I had always loved radio, and the idea of helping get ordinary people's voices on the air. 'Just be back here at 11am. We'll edit them and get them ready to broadcast,' the presenter said.

It was game on, no time to think or prepare.

The sun was shining brightly on the hilly streets of Derry as I ran towards town, equally nervous and excited about my temporary status as a radio reporter. I knew Derry people weren't shy, but also that they don't suffer fools and wouldn't be slow about telling me to get stuffed if I came at things the wrong way. The conflict had more or less ended, but there were still huge issues to address – a legacy of colossal hurt, trauma, deprivation and mistrust. People on all sides had lost loved ones or been imprisoned, been injured or suffered as a result of the violence that was part of life here from the early 1970s until the late 1990s.

Thinking back to that awful period in history, I wasn't sure what views might greet me here on the streets of Derry all these years later.

Within minutes of walking down the street, I met Cara. 'The people of Derry are always very positive,' she said. 'From the strife and troubles we've had in the past we sort of always move on and work for a better future, so the hope is always going to come from the people.'

I ventured down to the new Peace Bridge, which crosses for 235 metres over the mighty River Foyle. Designed as a symbolic handshake, this striking modern structure connects the city's two tribes – the majority 'Nationalist' (or Catholic tradition) on the 'Cityside' with the minority 'Unionist' (or Protestant tradition) on what's known as the Waterside.

On the bridge, I met Simon, a young father spending time with his son. He seemed to share Cara's optimism. 'We're sitting on the new Peace Bridge at the moment; this is evidence of hope and opportunity and communities coming together to enjoy what we have, this beautiful riverside city. I'm certainly a convert to investing in Derry, Derry-Londonderry.'

The next person to appear on my horizon was an American woman, Linda, who was slowly making her way down the street on crutches.

'Oh, hope can come from anyplace,' she said. 'You look around you, the fact that you wake up in the morning, that's hope. Especially in my condition. I've been waiting for the past three years to get a hip replaced, and it's getting to the point where I can't get out of bed in the morning. So if I can get out of bed, feed the animals, that's hope. I recently finished the Foyle Hospice fundraising walk. There's hope inside everybody. You can find inner strength anywhere, it's just not always where you think.'

After a few more interviews in the city I found myself venturing back to the Peace Bridge, where I met Rory.

'There's no quick answer to that question, because it's very deep. Hope for me is very important, because there is a lot of darkness and negativity in the world. Negative emotions too,' he told me. 'I have to believe that there is something worth getting up for, or living for, and it's people – to actually enjoy relationships with people and giving and receiving.'

Rory was relatively young, but clearly a guy who had reflected on these matters.

'It's easier to live in ignorance if you don't have to consider the horror that exists in the world. It's more comforting to believe that things are being taken care of, and you don't need to think about things. As they say, ignorance is bliss. But every person, I think, has a responsibility to the future, to future generations. We have to open our eyes to what's going on. I think awareness is key to change – it's the light, you know. If things remain hidden, then nothing gets done about it, nothing changes. I'm starting to sound like Gandhi now,' he concluded, smiling.

I arrived back at the radio station out of breath, with just moments to spare until I had to hand over the files in preparation for broadcast.

'Are ya all right there, Ruairí? Ya look a bit whacked!' one of the team shouted over, laughing at my bedraggled state.

Catching my breath, I handed over the recordings and went outside to call Susan while they went through them.

'You're what? You're doing interviews for the BBC? Well, whatever you're up to, it sounds like you're enjoying yourself,' said Susan, recognising the child-like excitement in my voice. 'I'm delighted for you, Ruairí. Enjoy every minute of it.'

Susan's constant encouragement made things so much easier, but I was starting to miss her. I was due to meet her in Kildare in a couple of days for a wedding, so we'd be able to catch up then.

'Ruairí, the vox pops are great,' one of the crew members remarked after I ended my call. 'Do you want to go on air and talk about them?'

'Absolutely,' I responded, grateful for the opportunity to go on the same show two days in a row.

The interview was perhaps the best I had experienced in almost 15 years of engaging with the media. The presenter was fully immersed, listening deeply, and taking his time as we explored the issues. This is all too rare in the fast-paced media world, which doesn't always reflect the reality of so-called ordinary people.

I thanked the staff at the radio station for their generous support and explained that I'd be back to collect my rucksack in a couple of hours. They had gone out of their way by having me on air not once, but twice, airing some of my vox pops, storing my bag, feeding me and making me feel hugely welcome.

Down on Great James Street at the Cultúrlann Uí Chanáin Irish language and cultural centre, I met up with my old school friend Barry who was staying over the border in nearby Inishowen for a few days.

'Man, you'd probably be as well getting out of the north today,' said Barry, reminding me that tomorrow was the Twelfth of July. This was a day when many in the Unionist community celebrated the 1690 Battle of the Boyne, marking Protestant William of Orange's (King Billy) victory over the forces of Catholic leader King James II.

It was often a very tense day, and many from the Catholic tradition chose to stay at home or travel to Donegal or elsewhere south of the border.

'It used to be a lot worse, there'd be riots and all sorts of trouble, but things are improving with each year. To be honest, I wish we could have a more normal society. I don't want my kids to have to grow up with all that crap,' exclaimed Barry.

We were in danger of being overtaken by a gloomy topic, but it was hard not to be upbeat in the vibrant atmosphere of the Cultúrlann centre. The place seemed a beacon of hope in a city that had been battered and bruised for centuries. The centre represented what's possible when individuals dare to dream, when communities come together, and when passion and hard work converge to make change happen. Rather than lament the loss of the Irish language, activists here had taken matters into their own hands and created a world-class building with an emphasis on promoting the Irish language as part of our shared heritage.

'That's the thing about people north of the border,' said Barry. 'They know how to get things done. It would be great to see more places like this south of the border.'

He was onto something. The atmosphere was modern and welcoming, a place where people could begin or continue their journey with the Irish language. Things were changing down south, with a new language movement emerging, but I'd never seen anything like the Cultúrlann centre in the Republic where Irish is supposedly the first official language. I had come across a similar centre in West Belfast and it reminded me how different the approach to the language was up north – much more community-driven.

Perhaps that's because the Irish identity is perceived by many to be under threat in the north, or because the State doesn't support Irish language development as much. The fact that students north of the border don't get daily Irish language lessons, unlike their southern cousins, spurs people to take action. The result has been an energetic grassroots language movement that inspires hope for the future of the language.

Back at the radio station, I used a spare studio for an interview with RTÉ Radio before asking advice on where I might hitch on to later that evening.

'Well, tomorrow is a big one,' said one of the guys. 'You know it's the Twelfth, so there's a big focus on the marches, and it'll be hard to get around or do anything else. If you do end up staying, be sure to pop up to our outside broadcast and give us your view on it all.'

The more I thought about it, the more this sounded like a rare opportunity, a chance to experience a Twelfth of July parade firsthand. I had wanted to head deeper into mid-Ulster the next day and then work my way on to Kildare to meet Susan the day after. The logistics could get messy if I stayed, but I was on this trip to listen and learn. Learning more about the other main tradition on our island would be an important part of that experience. Barry had texted saying his friend on the Waterside had offered me somewhere to stay, so there were no excuses.

I now had some proper breathing space to hang out with Barry. We didn't get to see each other as much as we wanted, so this was a good opportunity to reminisce and catch up.

'Have you seen that Derry record store in the news at all?' asked Barry. 'It used to be part of the HMV chain of shops, but it closed down, and the staff, who are real music lovers, took it over and renamed it WAH.'

The newly opened shop was booming, thanks in part to the publicity following a legal letter from HMV. The news had gone viral, and people all over the world were supporting the lads. It was a good-news story about turning adversity into opportunity, with a nice portion of cheekiness thrown in for good measure.

At the shop I met one of the owners, a former assistant manager for HMV. He explained that after losing his job when the company pulled out of Northern Ireland, he wasn't sure what to do next in a city that had long suffered high unemployment rates.

'We decided we'd do something for people left behind with no internet who wanted to get DVDs and CDs. So, we decided to open something locally. Given HMV pulled out of Ireland, we decided to call the store HVM as a marketing tool. HMV didn't like it. They said it was a copyright issue, so we flipped the letters upside down, and it's now WAH – which is kind of local slang for "what?" It came about because a customer we were telling about the situation said, "H M wha?" So it's a local business, a start-up, a cottage industry. We hope to maybe employ some guys who were made redundant. Hopefully that's the end of it with HMV. *WAH* shouldn't cause any issues with the big guys across the water.'

————

As evening set in, we wandered around the Bogside area looking at the murals and standing on the site where, on 30 January 1972, thirteen civilians were killed by British soldiers, on what became known as Bloody Sunday. Another later died in hospital. The marchers, led by the Northern Ireland Civil Rights Association (NICRA), had been demanding an end to widespread discrimination against Catholics, and an end to internment, which involved mass arrests and imprisonment without trial.

Bloody Sunday was a tipping point in modern Irish history, a moment when many ordinary people decided peaceful protest for civil rights wasn't going to be enough. In the days that followed, people queued up to join the IRA.

At the famous Free Derry Corner, the mural 'Welcome to Free Derry' was painted pink in solidarity with the city's LGBTQ+ community. Powerful gestures like this serve as an important reminder that republicanism in its truest form is about promoting the values of a republic, a state that values and cherishes all citizens.

It was late, and Barry needed to get going. I was sad to say goodbye. He had been the staunchest of supporters for the hitching project, encouraging me to do it when others were casting doubts on its purpose or viability.

Barry is a big-hearted fella who loves family, friends and the buzz around weddings and occasions. A couple of years previously, he had given up his job because he couldn't bear the thought of sending his young daughter and son off to childcare each day. It was a brave move, financially challenging for him and his wife, Marie, a teacher. But they made it work, cutting back on non-essentials and investing everything they could in the care of their children.

'Oh, before we go. I meant to ask. How are the wedding plans coming along?' he asked.

'Well, Susan and I have taken our first vow, and that's not to get stressed about the whole thing.'

'It's going to be epic, man, I know it. I can't wait,' said Barry, as we stood by the iconic mural. Seeing his genuine excitement, I realised how lucky I was to have a good pal like this to encourage me on, not only on this hitching trip, but also in my next big adventure: marriage.

He was the perfect choice to be my best man. We had been friends since we were four years old in dungarees and dodgy haircuts on our first day at St. Michael's National School in Cootehill.

Special moments need to be seized, and this was one of those. So there, standing beside the pink mural, I popped the question and we hugged as Barry let rip a joyous roar of 'Bring it on!'

9

The Orange, the Green and the White

Derry

THE NEXT MORNING, I WANDERED BLEARY-EYED AROUND the Waterside part of Derry, where crowds were starting to gather for the Twelfth of July festivities. In the distance, I could hear the sound of 'The Sash,' the drum-filled anthem of the Orange Order, a Protestant fraternal organisation established in 1795. The anthem celebrates King William III's victory over King James II and is generally considered antagonistic to people of Catholic backgrounds.

Growing up just south of the border, some of our teachers instilled in us the sense that the British were oppressors, the source of Ireland's woes for hundreds of years. Although 26 of Ireland's 32 counties had achieved independence in 1922, the north was still under British rule.

I had come a long way from my first year of university in Scotland when I hung an Irish flag above my bed and carried around all sorts of fears and foolish prejudices. Within weeks of starting university, I was partying with my new, northern Protestant pals and coming to understand the role of ignorance and 'othering' in keeping people apart.

However, the Orange Order added another dimension to this conversation. To many people, the Orange Order represented oppression. Critics claimed it was prejudiced against not only Catholics, but also women and people from the LGBTQ+ community. I had had no direct experience with the Orange Order, although several of my pals at university celebrated on the Twelfth of July. Other Protestant pals, those who didn't particularly identify as Unionist, weren't so keen on the Twelfth, feeling it misrepresented them. I had only witnessed their marches on television, and from my recollections, they appeared hostile and inflammatory. I had therefore always looked upon the Orange Order with a degree of suspicion. It was going to be an interesting day.

As I made my way closer to the centre of the festivities, the beating drums grew louder. The streets were packed with families setting up deck chairs and picnic blankets as they jostled for prime positions to watch the parade. Children's laughter mixed with drums and flutes. The band assembled, row after row, men in military-style uniforms with historic-looking crests, peaked hats, and impeccably shiny shoes. Everywhere I looked were Union Jack flags and bunting; a reminder that despite all the changes in recent times, identity still mattered here.

'You're still with us then? I hope it's going well,' came a voice with a distinct Derry accent from behind me. It was a woman I had met during the previous day's interviews. 'You should chat to that fella there, the Grandmaster,' the woman suggested. 'He's the top guy in charge of all of this, the head of the Orange Order.' My eyebrows raised in slight disbelief as I considered the situation I had arrived into.

'Emmmm, right, yeah, I suppose I might as well while I'm here,' I replied. However, as I stood debating how best to approach the man, I wasn't so sure. My old prejudices came bubbling to the surface as I recalled a memory of Unionist leaders Ian Paisley and David Trimble on the news in 1995, triumphantly marching hand in hand as part of an Orange march through a Catholic neighbourhood in Portadown. They were surrounded by hundreds of shouting supporters, seemingly taking the local people under siege. It was a defining moment in the conflict and unleashed a summer of riots that tipped things to the point of near civil war.

I set my memory aside and approached the Grandmaster through the crowd. He looked sternly ahead until I reached him. 'Do you mind if I ask you a few questions?' I said as tried to block out the surrounding noise.

'No problem,' he replied in a soft yet serious voice.

'Today is the highlight of our year,' he explained. 'We're celebrating the 323rd anniversary of the victory of King William at the Battle of the Boyne. It's very much a family-orientated day, and we have bands and parades. It's very important to keep our Orange heritage and culture going and we're delighted that there's so many people out here today to help us do that,' he told me.

I asked him about the tensions surrounding Orange parades and the fact that many Catholics feel threatened or offended by them. 'There's no problem living side by side,' he responded. 'I live and work alongside Roman Catholics. It's not a problem as long as we all respect each other. We believe in civil and religious liberty for everyone, and we practice that as well.'

I would have loved to hear more. To ask why they were celebrating the victory of one religion over another and why this organisation didn't allow Catholic, female or LGBTQ+ members. Members were even forbidden from entering Catholic churches. Surely there was a contradiction there when it came to humanitarian values and civil liberties. Alas, my questions would have to wait. The Grandmaster informed me that it was time for him to go, and bid me farewell as the strengthening drums indicated the parade was about to begin.

I was on my own again, standing in a sea of orange, the drums beating harder and harder as the parade started to move. I strolled along the edges, trying my best to look at ease in the midst of thousands of people. Grandparents, parents and children mingled with excitement and tucked into flasks of tea and homemade sandwiches. It was a sight far from the scenes I'd grown up viewing on television: the firebombs, riots and alcohol-fuelled taunting. This was a genuine family day out for most.

'I think there's a real move to rebrand today as a kind of Orange-fest, away from the political and religious connotations,' a woman at a food stall told me. I could see what she meant, but with the flags and emblems flying around me, I wondered how those connotations could be avoided. Some were held proudly by tough-looking men in paramilitary-style uniforms. How was I supposed to feel at ease with this? Yes, I got the fun, family picnic atmosphere, but there was also an edge that was difficult to ignore. What about the fact that this holiday made half of the north's population feel excluded, intimidated or insulted? I wasn't entirely sure how to reconcile the competing perceptions.

I made my way up towards 'the field,' as the locals referred to it, where teenagers kicked footballs around, people lined up for fast food, and a preacher prayed with a small group of mostly elderly people in a tent. Behind me, I spotted a journalist interviewing people about what the Twelfth of July meant for them. He wasn't settling for stock answers from people who said they were here to 'celebrate our Protestant culture'. He challenged them, asking them what they meant by 'Protestant culture'.

'It's what our parents and grandparents did, these marches, and the drums, we need to honour all of that,' one young woman responded. I understood that human desire to carry forward the torch held aloft by our parents, but I wondered if perhaps it was time for all of us to pause and ask what torches we were carrying.

I wandered around the field a bit more, taking in some of the sights and sounds. I chatted with a young man in costume whom I had assumed to be an Orangeman. It turned out he was a young Catholic actor playing a theatrical role and this was his first time ever at an Orange parade. He explained that identity was an evolving thing for him and many of his friends – that his girlfriend was Protestant, his best friend was Protestant, and while he saw himself as Irish, he had also grown to feel part of a new Northern Irish identity.

'I've always been a strong believer in not necessarily being part of the UK, but not really wanting reunification,' he said. 'Why would we want to throw away our education and healthcare systems? Perhaps we should be looking at making ourselves an independent identity. Northern Ireland should be northern Irish. By coming to things like this here today, I can see the culture from both sides. It's not my tradition, but it's interesting. These are all people who are now firmly northern Irish.'

I thanked the actor and went to check my phone when a tap on the shoulder interrupted me. 'Ruairí, we were wondering if you were around,' said a guy from the BBC, out of breath. 'Are you up for doing something on air? We have William Hay from the Democratic Unionist Party here – he's the Speaker of the Northern Ireland Assembly and a proud Orangeman. You'll be on air with him to give your views. Are you up for it?'

It had been a strange day, enjoyable in parts but challenging, and I tried to summarise it for the radio interview. 'Yes, there are issues that I find hard to swallow, what I see as old prejudices, but I can see too that there is a genuine aspect to this beyond division. There is a desire for people to come together and celebrate their culture and heritage and it's clear most people here are just here for a good day out with the families. I've met some great people today, and ultimately I know we've more in common than what sets us apart, something we need to remember as we build towards a better future for all on this beautiful island.'

Interestingly, as the day had progressed, I was reminded more and more of the St. Patrick's Day parades I had grown up with. While those were awash with green, this parade celebrated the orange portion of the Irish flag. The flag's green and orange stripes represented the Catholic and Protestant traditions, but the white stripe – the stripe whose hue has yet to be the star of any parade – represented the hope for peace between them. Given all the conflict of the past and the potential for more, it felt immensely important to hold a space for this white stripe.

———

I love percussion, but I had reached my fill of the relentless drumbeat that continued to ripple through the air. A buildup of poor sleep was leaving me irritated, and I needed to get moving. I had failed to make plans for my next passage and was realising that this could get tricky. Susan's cousin was getting married the next day in Kildare, and I had promised her I would make it, assuming I'd be much further along by now. 'No probs, love, just wrapping up here. I'll see you in the morning,' I had texted Susan while realising that it was now after 7pm and my chances of making it back to Dublin were diminishing by the second.

'With all the parades and the public holiday, it's just a bit messy and I don't fancy your chances, to be honest,' said a friendly-looking policeman when I asked him about my hitching prospects. *Oh, great,* I thought, imagining Susan flying solo at the wedding tomorrow and explaining to her family that I wasn't there because I was too busy hanging out with Orangemen up north.

10

On Home

Dublin to Kildare . . . and Back Again

I WOKE UP BESIDE SUSAN, AS THOUGH STILL IN THE depths of a blissful dream. It was so lovely to find myself in my own bed in Dublin, albeit with the orange drums still ringing in my ears. I snuggled up to Susan and fell asleep again until she woke me an hour later with tea and toast. 'You'd think I had been off cycling around the Alps, I'm that tired,' I told her through a yawn. I couldn't understand it. Maybe it was all the talking, or rather the listening, and the limited downtime I'd had.

Still, I couldn't complain. The sun had miraculously resisted cloud cover, I had visited some amazing places, and people were sponsoring me through online donations to do what I love. 'A paid hitching holiday sounds good to me,' someone had remarked, half in jest.

I wanted to beat myself up about catching the bus to Dublin the previous night, but I couldn't be bothered. What was the point? The only rules for my trip were self-created, and I wasn't pretending to be a hitchhiking puritan. Yes, I had cheated, but it was worth it. I managed to catch up on my blogs on the four-hour bus journey from Derry and arrived into Dublin City at midnight. It meant I had time to sleep, iron a shirt, and chill a bit before the drive to Kildare.

Susan and I took a morning walk over the Wooden Bridge onto Bull Island, up into the soft, rolling sand dunes of Dollymount Strand; a view of our beloved Howth Head peninsula to one side and the iconic red-and-white-striped Poolbeg chimney stacks near Dublin City to the other. It had been a hectic few days and here in familiar territory, I could feel myself relaxing with every breath. I decided to jump into Dublin Bay, the cold pulsating through my bones and leaving me reinvigorated and ready for the day.

'I hear you're in the *Irish Times*,' read a text from my brother, Seán Óg, after I had emerged from the water. 'Where are you today?' I had totally forgotten about the article, but Seán Óg's text reminded me to pick up the paper on the way back home. There I was, my big, bearded head on the front page under the headline, 'Hitchhiker's Guide to the National Mood'. I turned to the article and discovered a lengthy piece, alongside the picture from my photo shoot in Sligo. It was a strange sensation, reading about my trip while technically still on it. But I felt I had tapped into something special and it was important to share it.

'What's that you're wearing around your neck?' Susan asked, pointing at the photo. It was the necklace Simona had given me before we parted. I had put it on immediately after she gave it to me and had totally forgotten about it during the photo shoot. *I wonder if they're still in the country*, I thought. *It'd be funny if they picked up the paper and she saw her necklace in the national media.*

I texted Marco and 20 minutes later got a reply: 'Hi Ruairí, we are at the airport, in the departures ready to go home to Italia. It was great to travel with you. Please come visit us in Roma.'

'Go get the *Irish Times* if you can,' I replied.

Five minutes later, another text from Marco: 'We are on the airplane. We have the paper. We see the photo and you are wearing the necklace! We love it! Very good to see you again. Ciao my friend.'

———

Back at the house I shined my shoes and donned a suit, transforming myself from rugged hitchhiker into respectable wedding guest before we set off for the celebration.

Down in County Kildare, we parked up at the country estate where Susan's cousin Deirdre and her partner Sam were to be married later that day. The mansion, a remnant of colonial times, was on the outskirts of town, surrounded by woodland and walls. It immediately reminded me of Bellamont House back in Cootehill – another impressive palatial house from that era. While I was growing up, this house was of huge interest to me, not so much due to its impressive Palladian architecture, but more so because of what it symbolised.

Cootehill itself was renamed from the Gaelic Muinchille, meaning 'the sleeve' (a reference to its hilly location amid the forests), after Thomas Coote – an English Cromwellian colonel who married Frances Hill from Hillsborough. For me, the town's name was a reminder of a time when its inhabitants existed to serve the needs of an imposed master, who generally lived in the local 'big house'. In my teens, I realised that some entrances to the town's forest were locked so that the estate owners could have the sprawling woodlands and lakes to themselves.

Many of the old houses on colonial estates have fallen into disrepair. Often their owners – British, Anglo-Irish, or others who have come into money – keep them going, hiring them out for weddings or festivals. While the culture of landlordism is still with us, opening the gates of these impressive buildings and estates to the masses feels like modest but positive progress towards healing historical divisions.

'Come on, Ruairí, it's a wedding day, never mind all that,' Susan said as we walked onto the grounds of the Leixlip Manor Hotel, former residence of the Earl of Lanesborough. I had been rambling on about the past and forgetting the present. Susan was right, of course; this wasn't a day for droning on about history, it was a day for making history – a day of love, fun and celebration.

'Ladies and gentlemen, please take your seats,' called the celebrant as we joined the other guests among the estate's stunning gardens. It was my first time at a non-church wedding, and I was intrigued. Most Irish weddings were held in churches out of tradition, but things were changing fast. Likewise, Ireland was an increasingly secular and diverse country, and the wedding reflected this. Deirdre, the bride, was from Dublin, and Sam, whom she met in Dublin, was the son of Sri Lankan immigrants to the UK. Their guests, many of whom had travelled from England, reflected a diversity that wasn't a strong feature of the Ireland I grew up in.

The ceremony, which Deirdre and Sam had designed themselves, was officiated by a celebrant but was non-religious. It felt relaxed, yet every bit as sacred as a church wedding. The celebrant offered blessings of love, making everyone present feel welcome. Susan's aunt Anna, a Catholic nun who had once worked in Ethiopia, read a selection of poetry by Rumi, the Persian Sufi mystic. The blending of cultures and the personalised ceremony fostered an atmosphere of togetherness, and we basked in Deirdre's and Sam's love for each other.

Later, I wandered around the grounds and got chatting to a woman about my age who seemed keen to talk about my trip and his thoughts on Ireland. 'I'm sick of it, Ruairí,' she said with an air of weariness. 'We're busting our asses working two decent jobs to support our mort-gage and childcare costs, but it never seems enough. We keep getting hit with sneaky taxes, and we're barely hanging in there. It's so unfair, those banker guys just running around feeding off us. I don't know what to do. Surely we have to do something about this?'

The pain in her voice was matched by the sadness in her eyes. The woman reminded me of so many others I knew who were buried in debt and struggling to find hope amid a political system that had failed them. Listening to her gave me a renewed sense of conviction that this trip was important – that these voices needed to be acknowledged and that the quest for hope was not just a personal one, but part of a collec-tive yearning.

If a voice of hope was needed, Sam's father, Mano Ponnuthurai, provided just that in the after-dinner speeches. This soft-spoken Sri Lankan had come to England with his wife in 1970, worked hard and made a good life for himself and his family. He spoke to the wedding guests of his love for Sam and Deirdre and the importance of show-ing kindness towards each other. 'And to the younger people here,' he concluded, 'never forget that you must work for fairness and justice in this world. It is so important, and I urge you to do all you can do,' he added, much to my delight. It was an all-too-rare invitation and challenge from an elder to the younger generation – one I would take with me as I continued on my journey.

———

My brief break from hitching was not quite finished. My back had started to cause me trouble, exacerbated by the heavy rucksack I'd been lugging around, and I had booked a Russian massage with Vasile Bria in Lucan, a neighbourhood in West Dublin.

Vasile was not new to me. I had first met the big, burly Moldovan massage therapist at the Body&Soul festival, where he developed a reputation as a miracle worker among revellers in need of a bit of repair work. Vasile seemed like the right man to help out on this pit stop.

Lucan is a neighbourhood rich with a diversity that still isn't common in many parts of Dublin. Many migrants had made their homes here due to the cheaper rents on the city's outskirts – people of African, Asian and Eastern European heritage.

Making my way through the dense housing estates towards Vasile's house, I thought about the recent rise in racial tensions across the country – no doubt not helped by skyrocketing unemployment figures that provoked people to search for someone or something to blame.

I wondered if Vasile had endured any negative experiences during his time in Ireland and asked him as he dissolved the hard knots in my shoulders. 'Oh, yes, I have had some small issues, but nothing bad, Ruairí,' he said with his strong Moldovan accent. While it was worrying to think of good people like Vasile and his family encountering racism, especially in a country with such a history of emigration, it was also encouraging to hear that his experiences were mostly positive. 'I had many problems in my own country too, you know. There is nowhere that is perfect, but Ireland is very special. I love it here, and it is now my home for my family.'

11

Life in the Balance

Dublin to Aughrim

IT SEEMED INCONCEIVABLE TO ATTEMPT TO TRAVEL around Ireland and ignore Dublin City, the undeniable centre of economic, political and cultural activity on the island. With almost 2 million people in the Greater Dublin Area, the region accounts for approximately 40 per cent of the republic's population and over 50 per cent of its economic activity. Yet despite being Ireland's biggest city, Dublin's not all that big. I often bump into people I know on the street, as one might in any small town.

I had been invited to do a few radio interviews in Dublin, and so I seized the opportunity to stay another day and tap into the pulse of the city. When I arrived at the first radio studio the next morning, the office was buzzing with electricity and adrenaline – staff ran from one place to the next, typing, making calls, and otherwise contributing to the constant feed of news stories. The energy was unlike anything I'd witnessed so far on my travels.

I sat on a couch preparing for my turn. 'What are you going on to talk about?' asked a Canadian man across the waiting area. I told him about my trip and asked him about himself.

'I teach improvisation, or improv as it's commonly known,' John said, explaining people's growing appetite to get away from the juggernaut of modern life and have a laugh through the improvised games and workshops he delivered. 'When I first came to Ireland years ago, people were more relaxed, funnier, more spontaneous. Some of that got lost with economic growth, but I see it coming back now, and that's good.'

I liked the sound of that. I love the idea of Ireland learning from the socioeconomic progress of societies like Germany, Switzerland and the Scandinavian countries, but I'd hate to see us grow stiff and rigid and lose our sense of fun. I felt I had witnessed something of this over the years. Where once people had time for one another and for the occasional random encounter with a stranger, they now seemed to rush on to the next meeting or to fulfil overly scheduled work and social diaries. So-called progress seemed to come at the cost of time – time for thinking, time for family, friends, rest and play. It was perhaps no surprise that some countries were starting to look at national wellbeing and calculating Gross National Happiness, as opposed to the purely economic Gross National Product, as a true measure of their nations' success.

The idea of spontaneity was also appealing – the exhilaration, freedom and excitement that come from leaping without knowing what happens next. Albeit in a very different form, hitching was helping me rediscover this joy. It was allowing me to get away from the constant grind of planning, programming, checking off to-do lists and figuring things out.

It was as if the not-knowing was opening up space for more magic, for chance encounters, and incredible conversations. Rather than incurring anxiety from the absence of a plan or a lack of security, I felt more alive than I had in ages.

———

My radio interview was short and sweet, and afterwards I wandered over to the nearby French-style Metro Café, where I sipped on a coffee while contemplating my next move. Dublin was a different beast from other stops on this trip, marching to a much faster beat. I was curious about how people might respond to my questioning

'Well, let me say I heard you on the radio this morning,' replied the first person I stopped – a man in a suit on his way to work. The recognition caught me by surprise. 'You're the hitching guy, aren't you? You want to know about hope, about Ireland?' he asked.

'It's not looking too good. We're losing vast numbers of talented people to emigration, and the debt levels are impossible to service. An ageing population won't be able to service the pension fund. There's no other way but to revisit the possibility of burning the bondholders and getting rid of some of this illegitimate debt.'

It was interesting that the national debt kept coming up. The government had been elected on promises to cut us a new deal and then did everything in their power to spin that as an impossibility we now needed to forget. It seemed people weren't forgetting, nor should they.

My next conversation was with a 19-year-old student who was less pessimistic. 'Yeah, I know the economy isn't great, but there's always different ways of looking at things,' he suggested. 'I have a day off today and I'm going to spend it going around galleries and museums, nearly all of which are free. I think it's important to focus on the positive things and not to dwell on the negative aspects too much.' He bounced off happily to the beat of the music from headphones. I appreciated his calm and pragmatic reaction, which expressed a wisdom I wished I'd had when I was his age.

I walked down towards the Dame Street thoroughfare where lines of shoppers filed past people begging on the street and lying in doorways. Dublin had always had a large number of people who were homeless, but that number had increased significantly in recent years. Job losses, cutbacks to health and social services, and a lack of affordable housing had all contributed to the rising number of people without homes, including families, migrants, and those whose social support systems had broken down. Addiction to alcohol and other drugs, as well as mental health challenges, were other factors contributing to the high levels of homelessness.

I wanted to hear these people's stories and share them with the world, but every time I went to approach someone, something held me back. I felt too voyeuristic, like I was tokenising their pain. I knew these folks needed food, money and shelter, not some hitchhiker guy attempting to exploit their tragedies so he could tweet about them. Of course, a meaningful conversation could be a powerful way to break through the prejudice and ignorance that allows people to write off fellow humans as 'scumbags' and 'junkies', demonstrating instead that those who are lost, injured or vulnerable need our love and support, not our pity or condemnation. But as much as I wanted to give voice to these issues, it didn't feel right. The balance between humanising and dehumanising was a difficult one to strike.

———

The flow of Dublin's pedestrian traffic brought me onto Grafton Street, and I soon found myself at the gates of Trinity College – a world away from the poverty just a few streets over. Trinity was founded in 1592 to educate Ireland's then principally Protestant ruling class and is still often associated with prestige and privilege. Yet despite its reputation for elitism, Trinity has long since opened its doors to others and broadened its representation of Ireland's wider society.

Standing by the entrance archway, I spotted a silver-haired man handing out leaflets promoting walking tours. I decided to see if he might be up for a chat. I learned that Tommy was the founder and editor of *History Ireland* magazine and had much to say on the question of hope.

'You have to see the current dysfunction in a historical context. Ireland has been dysfunctional for hundreds of years,' he told me. 'There's nothing new here. Many of our problems stem from the capitalist system, which has inherent contradictions. I like the eighteenth-century notion of democracy, of "liberty not licence", which talks about the need for people to take responsibility, to take ownership for some of the problems. The current Irish political system is based on clientism, where the politician does what appears to be favours for the electorate, and they get voted back in. This has to change,' he said, before leaving to meet his tour group.

Tommy's view echoed that of archaeologist Michael Gibbons on Inishbofin, but I liked his added commentary on the idea of 'liberty not licence'. While it's important to pursue individual meaning and purpose in the world, we must remember that the freedoms we enjoy come with responsibilities; our welfare as individuals is reliant on our collective wellbeing and that of the planet.

In the wide-open cobbled courtyard on the Trinity campus, I met a visiting academic from South Africa. 'Look at apartheid. It has ended. It is proof that hope is always possible, but you must work for it,' she said as we got to talking about Nelson Mandela. It was perhaps fitting that Mandela would surface in conversation on this day, as news of his impending death had recently surfaced in the media. 'His story is one of hope if ever there was one,' she added.

From the courtyard I wandered towards the steps of the modern, flat-roofed Berkeley library building. 'Oh, I think we're in a good place, actually,' said a young student I met there. 'The economy is bouncing back and as for climate change, Ireland is well placed to handle that.' He spoke with a confidence that seemed out of sync with what so many others had to say. Was it because he was right? Or perhaps lived in a different reality, or had different news sources and perspectives? Most people thought the economy was stagnant, while austerity had drained away our public infrastructure. But while I could see how our interpretations of the economy might differ, I couldn't accept how Ireland was in a position to withstand the immense and immediate challenges of climate change.

The student's optimism, however, was shared by two lecturers I met on their way back from lunch. 'When you see things happening several times, you don't get too worked up about it. None of us are going to starve. We're taking another pay cut. It'll mean we're 20 per cent down on salary from a few years ago. Our pensions will be whacked. Our motto is just to drink more rosé wine. Do you not think it's just the media whipping all this up?' one of the lecturers asked.

'I'm from the west of Ireland,' he continued, 'and when I was growing up, half the kids in our school only saw their fathers for two weeks at

Christmas and another two weeks in the summer. The rest of the time they worked in England or Scotland or somewhere like that. Dublin was a foreign city. So, there's a long tradition of this. We got all inflated by the Celtic Tiger and people are behaving as if we've had generations of prosperity,' he concluded.

His colleague jumped in. 'I've huge sympathy for people with young families and mortgages.' she said. 'As far as emigration is concerned, during the Celtic Tiger it was called overseas experience; now it's called emigration. I wouldn't want to minimise the experiences for people. It's not too bad. It's going to be okay. Nobody is starving.'

She was right that things weren't that bad when compared with what was happening in places like Greece or Gaza. Nonetheless, the large numbers of homeless people I'd seen on the streets that morning pointed to a different story. I found it hard to agree with this somewhat clinical view of a situation that was causing so many people to experience suffering.

My next conversation was with a Canadian teenager visiting Ireland on a high school trip. This was another good opportunity to get a view from the outside looking in. 'I've only been here a day or two, but I really like Dublin so far,' she said. 'The people are pretty easy-going, but it does seem there's a hell of a lot of drinking going on, and I was surprised at the number of homeless people around. In general, I have a good impression of Ireland. North America is different; it's all forward motion, a rat race to nowhere, and it's making people ill. The pressures on students are unreal. We leave university drowning in debt.'

On the subject of creating a more hopeful world, the student had an impressively well-rounded view. 'People have to keep some morals in line and strive to make the world a better place. That's all you can do to keep yourself happy, and others. I'm not necessarily talking about religious morals, just to keep some social principles – kindness to other people, not to be always selfish, be honest, be truthful to yourself.'

———

After a quick lunch with my old school pal Stephen, I wandered through the crowded, cobbled streets of the Temple Bar area. On the edge of

Temple Bar Square, I stumbled upon a young, barefooted bohemian-looking fellow selling his self-published book of poetry in the street. He looked like he was in his element, reading poems as tourists, shoppers and workers streamed by in the afternoon sun.

'Yeah, back a few years ago I was struggling and went to Spain, and the words flew out of me, so I made this book,' he told me. I asked him about his vision for Ireland. 'I think we need a fair system of income distribution, a normalised distribution of income,' he posited. 'The distribution of income in our society is highly skewed. This forces the multitude into poverty. We need more of a merit-based system – not necessarily everyone earning the same amount, but everyone aspiring to having a normal life. That way we can restore balance to society. I'm hopeful so long as people can wake up to the reality of life, get back to nature. I've been living a more natural life. I think the key to life is in getting back to Mother Earth.'

His bare feet, an unusual sight in Ireland, seemed to be part of his freedom philosophy. 'It makes practical sense. I see people walking around on a swelteringly hot day with shoes, and they must be very hot inside. You can see people walking around with big runners and big socks and they're clearly not comfortable in their lives. I can assure you that not wearing shoes is highly preferable to wearing them. It's just one of those things, part of our psyche. We're led to believe that we need all these extra contraptions in our lives when in fact we don't.'

While I wasn't particularly up for being barefoot in the city, part of me envied the man's sense of freedom and lack of inhibitions. I'd always romanticised the life of the travelling poet, moving from town to town, absorbing new inspirations, and paying their way through poems. I had read Kerouac when I was younger and thought there was something electric about how he saw life as a wild adventure to be lived fiercely and fully. Then there is Pat Ingoldsby, Ireland's oft-overlooked national treasure, an ageing word-warrior known for sitting on the street selling his witty, fun-filled poems that capture the madness of daily life. It can't be an easy road to follow, but at least people like him stay true to themselves and their gifts.

I said goodbye to the poet and ventured towards the television studios on the outskirts of Dublin, where, before I knew it, I was in a dressing room getting makeup applied to my face. I smiled, thinking how far removed this moment was from the beat-poet lifestyle I had been contemplating. The make-up artist wasn't shy about sharing her views as she powdered my face.

'Everyone has to have hope. If you don't, there's nothing. I've seen everything in here – harrowing stories, people having to emigrate, going to Australia and Canada. I wouldn't like it to happen to my family. I think the senior citizens have taught us a lesson about speaking out, and we should all get out there and say: "No more!" I think the Irish people have been beaten down by so many taxes. People can't take any more.'

Waiting to go on air, I got chatting to Maedhbh, a young teacher also scheduled to do an interview. 'I set up a support group for people suffering from Raynaud's phenomenon and scleroderma, which are autoimmune conditions where, respectively, your hands turn purple or white and your body overproduces collagen, irreversibly attacking healthy organs,' she explained.

'About 10 per cent of the Irish population have a small degree of Raynaud's phenomenon, and 2 per cent of that number usually also have scleroderma. Years ago, scleroderma could kill you, but now it can be treated. The main thing is to have support, so we organise talks and bring people together for conferences and local meetings and just build up solidarity.'

I asked her why she dedicated herself to supporting others. 'My diagnosis of scleroderma took about four years to get. I'm lucky mine is slow-moving, but I want to make sure no other girl with agonising pain [related to the disease] doesn't know what's going on. I want to help get in there before the panic sets in. Most of the women have spent their entire lives taking care of their husbands and their children and now their parents, and they need someone to take care of them,' she told me. 'The more proactive you are, the more in control you feel, and it's less like the condition is happening to you and more that you are living with it.'

Maedhbh's perseverance was admirable, and her support group a real testament to the kind of social solidarity that was holding the country together. Even in the bleakest of circumstances, people often demonstrate a remarkable capacity to band together.

———

There was much more I wanted to do in Dublin and many invitations I couldn't respond to, but I knew I should press on. True to the spirit of improvisation, I wasn't exactly sure where I wanted to land next, but I knew I wanted to head south. As I contemplated my options, the phone rang. It was another newspaper photographer requesting another staged photo. 'I'm in Dublin now and on my way to Aughrim in Wicklow,' he said.

This was the perfect opportunity to get out of Dublin, and an hour later, I was on my way to Aughrim with the photographer, stopping for a quick photo op that I prayed would go unnoticed. As we turned off the main road at Kilmacanogue and ascended into the Wicklow Mountains, I could feel my body and mind relax, the green fields and peaceful valleys offering a solitude Dublin had drowned out.

Along the way, the photographer shared with me his own experiences: the challenges of a negative equity mortgage and exorbitant childcare costs that were crushing many young families. 'The pressure is unreal. I don't know how we're going to do it, but something drastically needs to change,' he said.

After he dropped me off in Aughrim, I got a bit of lunch before wandering around the small town. Aughrim is one of those places where the ghosts of history peek out from behind the trees and buildings. Hidden in the Wicklow hills, it is situated in a valley where the Ow and Derry Rivers meet to form the Aughrim River. A plaque on the bridge in this former granite-mining town commemorates Anne Devlin, a Wicklow woman who was imprisoned and tortured for her involvement with revolutionary leader Robert Emmet and the United Irishmen in the years surrounding the 1798 rebellion.

Paul, a friend of a friend who lived in Aughrim, had offered to meet me later that afternoon at the monument in the middle of the village to take me on a special tour. 'How's it going, Ruairí?' he asked as he pulled up in his van. 'Great to meet you. Hop in.'

We stopped off at a nearby native woodland and ventured uphill on a network of small, tree-lined paths as birds sang overhead. 'This recreational woodland area was protected and developed by local volunteers,' Paul told me. 'It's a reminder of how people can get things done when they need to. I have a few plans myself for the area that I'd like to see happen,' he added, before being interrupted by the revving of a motor.

On closer investigation, we found a group of teenagers in an old four-wheel drive that they had been driving up and down the hill for fun. They had burned out the engine and were now panicking over what to do. A woman who lived nearby came running over. 'Oh, I'm bloody sick of them. They have us tormented, driving around at all hours and making a racket.' The teenagers seemed embarrassed by their predicament, and Paul offered them a few words of caution and advice on showing a bit more respect for the area.

Are there any youth clubs here, or is there much to do for local young people? I wondered, thinking back to my meeting with Barry, the youth worker in Oughterard.

'Not enough, to be honest, something we also need to be working on. There's a responsibility on parents and the teens themselves, but it's also up to the community to make a bit of an effort to help these young ones out so they aren't wrecking the place and getting themselves in trouble,' said Paul.

'These kinds of situations often remind me of an African proverb I once heard,' I replied. 'It goes that the child who is not embraced by the village will burn it down to feel its warmth.' Indeed, all over the country adults blamed teens for causing trouble, yet not enough was being done to create places where they could socialise constructively.

Paul and I met up with his housemate James and together walked over to a giant, seventeenth-century mill abandoned since the 1960s. The complex of tall, vast stone buildings beside the river, surrounded by a network of sheds, had once been the lifeblood of the town. Paul and James had an enthusiastic vision for bringing the old facility back to life as a hub for local renewal and community development. 'We could create green energy that could power the buildings and probably even the town. It could be a base for artists, craftspeople, food producers, theatre, small business start-ups, youth groups and a club for older people,' Paul described with a passion that could turn this type of dream into reality.

'It has the potential to create jobs, bring life back into the area and stop all the young people having to leave. It could be cooperatively owned, with local people as shareholders, giving them a real sense of ownership, pride and participation, and instead of just one or two people profiting, everyone would win. I know it sounds a bit out there, but there was a time when the co-op movement was huge in Ireland, and there's no reason we can't return to that. It's a no-brainer, but it does mean we need initial investment and support to get us started.'

As I looked at the cobweb-filled doorways, broken roof and weeds pulling the buildings back towards the earth, I could see why people might be sceptical about these two young guys and their big dream. However, my own experience had taught me not to be dismissive of such idealism.

Talking to Paul and James reminded me of the conversations about the need for rural revival I'd had with my friend Keith in Ballyshannon back in 2004. We were full of ideas and energy, which we harnessed to create The Beehive as a cultural hub and base for Community Creations and SpunOut.ie.

At the time we had great allies, but we also faced the doubts of influential local agencies who appeared more focused on the potential of multinational companies than on seeing how a cluster of young, tech-driven start-ups like ours might bring considerable benefits to the area. We succeeded in gaining traction and creating jobs, but in the end, the pull to relocate to the city grew too strong to resist. Thinking back on it all, I hoped Paul and James would get the support they needed to manifest their vision.

Back in the lads' apartment, I met their friend Michelle, who suggested they weren't just dreamers. 'The Craic in the Granite festival proved what's possible, if you ask me,' she said, referring to a local arts festival the friends had recently organised. 'We just decided it was happening and, lo and behold, everything started to come together. Musicians, artists, local shops, so many people came on board. We did have one or two naysayers, but we proved them wrong. In the end, we had hundreds of people attending an entirely volunteer-run festival over three days. It was a massive boost to the local economy and local pride. It improved the sense of community spirit and really uplifted people. So many people are talking about it and asking, "What's next?"

'I got so much pride from it,' Michelle confessed as she put on her coat to leave. 'It gave me a huge sense of value. Yeah, it lifted me up, I have to say. I don't give a crap about mortgages or savings or loans anymore. It's all about walking out, breathing in the fresh air and being able to do whatever you want.'

'You might as well stay the night,' Paul suggested after we finished a tasty casserole. It seemed as good an idea as any, so I took him up on the offer.

We sat late into the night drinking tea and discussing a book the lads had been reading: *Who Owns the World: The Hidden Facts Behind Landownership*, by Irish-born investigative journalist Kevin Cahill, a former British soldier who previously acted as an advisor and researcher to a number of high-profile British politicians, including former UK Foreign Secretary Robin Cook. The book had obviously struck a chord with James and Paul, and they were both energised and angered by it.

'It looks at land ownership over the centuries,' James explained. 'This all goes back to the realm of kings and queens, aristocrats, rulers and serfs and why this is still relevant. It explores how poverty and wealth are connected, and how wealth has been traditionally determined by who owns land. Cahill says about 3 per cent of the world's population owns 97 per cent of the land. That's staggering eh? Even today, by holding the title to over 2.4 billion hectares all over the world, the largest landowner on Earth is technically the queen of England.

'Not that much has changed in over 100 years, and you can see this by looking at the big landowners of farms and estates throughout Europe. Cahill says they represent just 0.2 per cent of Europe's population but own 60 per cent of Europe and are subsidised by taxpayers through 60 per cent of the EU agricultural subsidy, which runs into billions of euros. Ultimately, most of the world's population is crammed into cities where people own very little, while the bulk of land is owned by the very wealthy,' he concluded.*

This was heavy stuff to process so late at night. I had studied my fair share of international history and politics and looked into the workings of bodies such as the World Trade Organisation, the International Monetary Fund, the Bilderberg Group and other powerful forces that influence our democracies. As such, I knew that there was a danger of falling into rabbit holes of cynicism, despair or even conspiracy when faced with a lot of the information that was out there. It was important to try to keep perspective while also contending with bitter truths.

Two o'clock came and went, and finally, everyone went to bed. I lay there with my head spinning as I tried to distill our conversation. Local versus global, darkness versus light – where to focus our energy? Should we ignore the dark forces operating at the global and national level and set about building new realities from the ground up? If we do, can we succeed, or will we ultimately have to dance to the tune of the dominant powers? Or do we invest in exposing and replacing undemocratic systems, and then set about building the alternatives? Maybe the answer lay somewhere in the middle, in a balance of proposition with opposition, resistance to injustice with the creation of positive alternatives.

---

* Kevin Cahill, *Who Owns the World: The Hidden Facts Behind Landownership* (Edinburgh: Mainstream, 2006).

12

The Hare's Corner

Gorey to Dunmore East

SIPPING MY MORNING COFFEE AT JAMES AND PAUL'S apartment, Colm Mac Con Iomaire's name kept surfacing in my mind. Colm is a professional musician – a founding member of legendary Irish indie rock band the Frames, and a world-touring solo violinist.

I knew Colm lived in County Wexford somewhere, just south of Aughrim, and the opportunity to hear from him seemed too good to pass up if it flowed. After messaging Colm to see whether he was available for a quick visit, Paul and James graciously delivered me in Gorey.

Colm's house, nestled among the rolling green fields of rural Wexford, was light, spacious and artistically decorated by his wife Sheila, a talented painter. He made up a nice, homegrown summer salad, and we sat down to enjoy lunch together. For a man who had travelled the world for 25 years and shared stages with some of the biggest names in music, he seemed comfortable living the simple life here in Wexford.

Colm's first solo album was called *The Hare's Corner*, after the old tradition whereby farmers left a section of their field to grow wild for the hare. In Irish mythology, the hare symbolises the Tuatha Dé Danann, or 'tribe of gods' – a group of pre-Christian deities. I love the idea of the hare's corner. It is a universal reminder that we all need to keep a hare's corner in our own lives: a space away from the world that's set aside for imagination, where the free spirit can roam, rest and dream.

'Ireland is in a wonderful stage of bloodletting and realisation, and the opportunity for change is great, but it needs to be seized,' Colm said after I asked him about the country's current turbulence. 'So I see it as something that is inspiring, rather than depressing. The Celtic Tiger period, and the abandonment of community and embrace of the individual consumer that it entailed, was one extreme in a cyclic pattern. What goes up must come down, and I think we've just hit the ground over the past few years. I think it's a case of, yeah, let's do things differently, and so I think that's the opportunity.

'We live in a time when secrets are impossible to keep anymore. So the truth is coming to light, left, right and centre, whether that be the Anglo Tapes or Wikileaks or pillars crashing around us – religion, and Catholicism and bankers. These had power because we invested power in them, so it's a case of realising our *own* power. I think that's where my optimism would be.'

Colm described what he saw as life's two basic choices: 'Either you can trust in your fellow human beings, that they're essentially good, that share your hopes and dreams of building a good world with, or there are people you need guard yourself from, in case they come and steal your stuff. I think we've been embracing that fear model, the one the Western world has been embracing for the past 20 or 30 years. Now we need to get back to the love model, which is about sustainability, tolerance, embracing diversity and celebrating of individual talent.'

After a satisfying lunch, Colm dropped me on the side of the R741, just up from a guy selling fresh strawberries and juice from a trailer, so I was well poised for refreshments if the hitching didn't go as planned. I situated myself under the shade of a giant oak tree and was soon aroused from my roadside daydreaming by Justin and his teenage son Andrew stopping to pick me up. The father-son duo said they'd drop me off down the road before they continued to the seaside village of Kilmuckridge. Like so many other Dubliners, they had a mobile home there where they spent as much time as they could each summer.

'Have you ever been to Kilmuckridge?' Justin wanted to know. I had heard of it but had never visited. 'I'm tellin' ya, you have to go there sometime. It's just the best. The rest of the family are down there now, and we're going down to join them. I've been coming down here for 37 years. Lots of my relations are here, and friends from my childhood. Everyone knows each other. The freedom is unreal. We escape the city each summer and the children roam free during the day. It's another world altogether. You'd love it,' he said with barely contained excitement.

'Ah feck it so, I'll spin down with you both if you don't mind,' I replied. I was in no rush to be anywhere in particular. We travelled down a bumpy country road as Justin continued to sing the praises of Kilmuckridge.

'I'm surprised one of the television channels hasn't caught on to the mobile home phenomenon and made a documentary about it,' he remarked. 'People have been doing it for years and years, where people buy mobile homes and caravans and jump ship from Dublin or the cities and move down into the country beside the sea. They spend two months. Fathers go up and work during the week and mothers stay down with the kids. It's a different way of life for two or three months of the year.

'Years and years ago, when it was really tough down here, in the 1980s, when there was no water or electricity, people would be coming down in hardship but still would always make the trip, and it could be lashing rain for the summer. You know, you could be barbecuing in the rain. But you still come down because of the beach and walks, and freedom. It becomes a way of life. You get friendly with people and they're friends for years. You'll get a taste of it when we get there,' he promised.

I asked Justin's teenage son Andrew how he felt about Kilmuckridge. 'I love coming down here, getting away from it all. When you come down here you are free, nothing to worry about, you just relax,' he replied, backing up his father's evangelical zeal, which grew stronger with every mile.

'Andrew doesn't have a curfew down here, once I know where he is. He's usually down at the beach, floating around. The same for me.

The minute I come down, I take off my watch. I don't want to know the time. It's just a gift.'

Arriving at the mobile home park, I could immediately see what Justin was talking about. Barefooted children ran around every which way, teenagers walked to and from the beach, and parents sat reading, chatting and listening to music. I was conscious that I was seeing Justin's special place at its best – under the sun's bright glare – but I could see the appeal. It reminded me of my childhood when my parents took us on camping and caravan holidays to Wexford, Cork and Kerry. There was something about the simple, back-to-basics approach, away from the bustle of airports and city traffic.

'Meet Ruairí, everyone, he's a hitchhiker we picked up,' Justin announced to his wife Ann-Marie and assorted family members as we stepped onto the deck of their mobile home. A moment of silence followed. Justin's family looked at him with confused stares, as if asking him, 'What have you done now?'

'Yeah, I'm hitching around Ireland, on my way to Wexford now,' I intervened, hoping to break the ice a bit, 'and Justin was telling me how great this place was. I was keen to have a look, but don't worry, I won't be bunking in with you or anything! I'll be heading off soon enough.'

'Great to meet you, would you like a drink or something to eat?' offered Ann-Marie, appearing much more at ease. I thanked her for her kindness, and before long, we were chatting like old friends, joking about the prospect of Justin joining me on my journey. Yet again, I felt refreshed and energised by the positivity and hospitality of the people I was meeting – their desire to help, to share and take part in my trip.

———

A local woman named Mary picked me up outside of Kilmuckridge and dropped me off several kilometres before Wexford Town, just opposite a memorial to the 1798 Battle of Vinegar Hill. It was in this battle that 20,000 British troops scored a decisive victory over the United Irishmen, a coalition of Presbyterian and Catholic revolutionaries that had risen up in a five-month rebellion during which 50,000 people were killed.

Standing there I got to thinking about the tides of history and how Ireland, it seemed, had never fully resolved its sense of statehood and nationhood. The woman who had dropped me off was testimony to this ambivalence – another mother whose son had recently left to seek a better life abroad.

'It breaks my heart, to be honest,' she said. 'I mean, I am happy for him in one way. He needed to get out of the house and start earning a living, but I miss him. I'm worried that he's going to end up staying away, meeting someone and having a family in Australia. What will happen then? The reality is I'd only see him again a handful of times for the rest of my life. There's only so much love you can share through Skype.'

I pondered whether things might have been different now for all those affected by emigration if the Irish Rebellion of 1798 had met with the same level of success as the French Revolution, which had begun a few years before it. What if the people of Ireland had forged ahead, and instituted liberté, égalité and fraternité as the principles at the heart of the nation? There was no doubt, based on all I was hearing on my travels, that these were principles yearned for by people everywhere.

———

I arrived into Wexford Town in the early evening, thanks to a lift from a chef who was bursting with entrepreneurial energy and opinion. 'You just have to give things a go. None of this sitting on your arse, getting State handouts and waiting for people to fix your life,' he admonished. 'There's no point blaming the government or just playing it safe. You just have to get out there, work hard, take risks. That's the way forward if you ask me,' he stated with conviction as we said our goodbyes.

Wexford looked stunning in the evening sun. Couples walked hand in hand by the waterside looking out on moored boats. I wandered the narrow, cobbled streets looking for a café where I could get some food and work on my laptop while I waited for Caroline, a local teacher who had contacted a friend of mine to express her interest in hosting me for the night.

It had been 12 years since I had first visited Wexford, back when I was living in Letterkenny and beginning to find my voice in the community. In the process of organising a fundraising concert to support refugees, I was asked if I would be interested in hosting a visiting tribesman from the jungles of West Papua who was scheduled to play music at the concert.

The next day, Sem arrived by bus with a traditional necklace of shells around his neck and a guitar strung over his shoulder. In a fitting reminder of the ubiquity of colonial struggles, he told the concert audience later that night how his native island of New Guinea had been divided between the British and the Dutch. When the Dutch left in 1962, the UN presided over a sham arrangement, known as the Act of Free Choice, which handed West Papua to Indonesia. Indonesia has since moved hundreds of thousands of its people there, welcomed Western mining companies onto the land, chopped down pristine rainforests and committed genocide against the native people.

You could hear a pin drop that evening as Sem sang Papuan songs that he couldn't sing in his homeland because they had been outlawed by the Indonesian government. The significance wasn't lost on us – these soulful songs of freedom ringing out over a land where once our language, music and beliefs were similarly repressed and forbidden. Sem and I became fast friends, and I took time off to bring him around the country to meet community groups and politicians. We ended up in Wexford for the Carnvaha festival, celebrating the twenty-fifth anniversary of mass anti-nuclear protests that had, against all odds, succeeded in preventing the construction of a nuclear power plant at Carnsore Point. I recalled the moment when the lead singer of the Hothouse Flowers, Liam Ó Maonlaí, called Sem up on stage to perform his traditional songs alongside the acclaimed Irish band. I was moved to tears watching this messenger from the Papuan jungle find shelter and solidarity among fellow musicians and an awestruck crowd.

Now, watching the sun set over Wexford 12 years later, I felt the spirit of that time rekindle inside of me.

———

Caroline and I hit it off immediately, and the next morning at breakfast we were straight into a conversation about life, politics, sport, music and Irish culture. In the background, a radio presenter announced that it was Nelson Mandela's birthday.

'I remember it all very well,' she said, remarking on the anti-apartheid struggle of the 1980s. 'I was out on the streets with the Wexford Anti-Apartheid Group supporting the Dunnes Stores super-market workers who were on strike, refusing to handle South African fruit at the checkout counters. Lots of people supported us, but so many didn't; they just ignored us or laughed at us. The same thing happens now with other campaigns. Look at the situation in Palestine. How can we pretend we don't know what's happening there? Mandela himself talked about that struggle when he was released. That's why we need activism; it puts on the pressure and says to people: "No, we can't just look the other way."

'We have been sold out to the top echelons of the capitalist system and nobody seems to see the damage this will cause to our citizens and the environment. We have to change our thinking, change our framework,' she told me. 'If I have to focus on one thing that needs to be changed, the ordinary people should not be paying the debts to German banks for money that we did not borrow. That just has to be taken on.

'I think we need to take on the health system,' she continued. 'As Martin Luther King said, the worst inequality is inequality in health, and our health system is unequal. Healthcare should be free for everyone. We pay our taxes, and there should be no barrier to people getting the healthcare that they need. Education as well. My father used to say that you judge a country by the state of its education and its health system. I'm a teacher, and I'm a little concerned about the narrowing of the curriculum to suit a particular economic model. So,

I would like to see Newman's idea of education and a university being embraced in the widest sense to cater for the intelligences of every child in the country.'

Despite her concerns, Caroline's remarkable optimism and sense of gratitude shone through as our conversation wound down. 'Well, you have to be hopeful for the future,' she said. 'I love my language. I love my music. I love going into Wexford Town and walking along the quay in the morning and people saying hello to you and hearing the chat of the older men. I love my country. You know, you have to see the good things in life and go with those. They are very often very straightforward. It's the simple things in life that are important.'

Caroline's friend Jane joined us a while later and shared her harrowing struggle to obtain adequate support for her two autistic children. 'It's a constant uphill battle,' she said with a look of weary determination. Jane was prepared to do anything to ensure her children could live a decent life. 'My family has lived in this area for the last 600 years. It's where I belong, it's where I like to live, but I am very disappointed in the people that have run this country consistently since my children have been diagnosed. They've been treated appallingly, we've been treated appallingly,' she said with disgust.

'At the height of the Celtic Tiger, when Evan was first diagnosed, I was standing on the main street in Wexford with a bucket trying to collect money to get occupational therapy for him at a time when the government didn't know what to do with their money, our money, but the last thing they would do was give it to us. The little bit that we did have, they've actually taken away from us. So I am extremely disappointed. I'm actually quite angry with the manner that we have been treated in our own country. We've had to fight tooth and nail for the last ten years for the little bit of help that we get, and the little bit of help that we get has been compromised time and time again.'

Jane's constant need to advocate reminded me of other parents I knew who seemed to be in a non-stop fight to secure resources and supports for their special-needs children. Parenting can be tough at the best of times, but I couldn't imagine the energy and effort these parents have had to invest, and the sacrifices they've made out of love. Why couldn't Ireland find the resources to provide the most basic services for people with special needs? 'The money's not there' is the usual refrain from policymakers, and yet they pour money into other questionable areas. As the adage says, you can judge the success of a society based on how it treats its most vulnerable.

———

Caroline drove me into Wexford town later that afternoon, and I planned to hitch onwards from there. As I thanked her for the amazing hospitality, I decided to go out on a limb and ask her if she happened to know a guy called Danny who used to run a campsite in town.

'Oh, Danny Forde. Yeah, I do. He doesn't run the campsite anymore, though. He got married and runs a haberdashery shop. It's just down there,' she said, pointing towards a small side street.

A minute later, I was explaining to Danny how we had met years before. 'Oh wow, Ruairí. Of course I remember you! You were with Sem back at the Carnvaha anti-nuclear festival. This is mad! I actually heard ya on the local radio earlier. You're hitching around Ireland, eh! Jasus, I didn't expect to be bumping into you like this.'

It was great to catch up with Danny, who shared with me his own journey of working for change. 'Yes, there has been lots of change in Wexford,' he said. 'I was elected on to the town council and I've been trying my best with that, but we're up against it. I'm involved in supporting local market traders to get a community market going. They're dismantling the town councils so power will be concentrated more centrally, which does nothing for local democracy. Still, you just have to do your best and chip away at it – but life is good.'

Fair play to him, I thought, admiring his patience, persistence and willingness to get involved in the messy world of politics.

It was now almost 8pm, and soon the roads would be too quiet for hitching. I had been thinking of heading to County Waterford, but this would be tricky now. Caroline had mentioned that I was welcome to stay another night, which was starting to seem like a good idea.

This was far from roughing it. People were messaging me on social media to tell me I was a great fella for 'walking across Ireland', but the reality was, with the combination of beautiful weather and gracious helping hands, things were flowing pretty smoothly, and there was very little walking required.

———

The following morning Caroline drove me to Ballyhack, where I hugged her goodbye and set off on the 15-minute ferry ride across the River Barrow to Passage East. The village looked radiant in the morning sunlight, nestled beneath a rocky hill as though hiding from the world. I disembarked from the ferry and made my way down the village's quiet streets.

A poster in a pub window advertised an event to support the families of three brothers who had recently drowned on a fishing trip. I made my way over to a park bench that looked out over the sea and sat thinking of the fishermen and their families. The poster spoke to the power of community solidarity so characteristic of rural Ireland in times of tragedy, and I hoped that those affected would find comfort in the healing power of this neighbourhood support system.

A phone call interrupted my thoughts. It was a local radio station requesting an interview in five minutes' time – an occasion that was becoming increasingly regular as the trip progressed. The only issue was a mild breeze interfering with the line quality. I asked them to call back and wandered around looking for shelter. When my phone rang again with 60 seconds to spare, I made a beeline for the public toilets and ducked behind the wall.

'Great to talk to you. Yes, I've just landed here in County Waterford,' I began, shaking my head at yet another amusing interview location. Later, my toilet-side accommodations led me to Adrian, a bearded, black-haired guy who was painting a fence. He had lost his job a few years ago, he said, and fallen into a rut at home. However, a local community employment scheme had helped him to get back on his feet.

'It gives me a basic wage, and I get out and about each day, talking to people. It's a reason to jump out of bed in the morning, and my confidence has improved,' he said, proudly surveying the fruit of his morning's labour. 'I'm far healthier, I now joke and laugh again. Things have brightened up. It's a real social opener. You get a pride in your own work, knowing that you are doing something that makes a difference.'

———

I headed to the main road leaving town and stuck my thumb out, eager to see where the trip would take me next. Soon, a man named Joe pulled over in a large van. I told him I was thinking of heading towards Waterford City, as I'd never been there. 'Waterford City is grand, but if you're only on a flying visit, Dunmore East is your best bet. I'm heading in that direction now if you want a lift,' he offered, and I hopped in.

'You know, I have a field there you can camp in,' Joe suggested, eager to help out. 'Well, there's a few people there now, friends of mine with their kids, but I'm sure they wouldn't mind you joining them.' I hesitated, recalling the looks on the faces of the Kilmuckridge family when Justin had announced my arrival.

'That sounds good, Joe, but I'm sure your friends have their own thing going on, and it might seem a bit odd me just landing in on them like that.'

'Nah, don't be silly. It'll be grand,' he assured me, and I had no good reason to refuse.

A few minutes later, we turned off the main road and headed down a narrow country lane, parking up by a gate to the flat green field that was to be my home for the night. 'See that old Traveller wagon down there?' asked Joe, pointing to a traditional wooden caravan that looked as though it belonged in a museum display. 'You can sleep in that for the night if you want. There's a mattress in it and everything, so there's no need to set up your tent. The others must be at the beach, but they'll be back later,' he assured me as he headed off.

I was left standing in the middle of the field, my only company a few tents, a camper van, a firepit and an assortment of children's bikes and toys. *What on earth are they going to think of a random stranger landing in the middle of their private summer adventure?* I wondered, sincerely hoping Joe wouldn't forget to let his pals know I was here.

I entered the wagon, dropping my rucksack on the floor and chuckling at the randomness of my new abode. I decided to go and explore while the afternoon sun was still out. After walking down a narrow dirt path for about five minutes, I reached a small beach of golden sand, nestled in a cove between two cliffs. Parents lay reading and tanning as their daredevil children jumped from the rocks into the clear sea. I wasted no time before jumping in myself.

'Amazing, isn't it?' asked a man who joined me on a walk up the cliff-side path after my swim. He was in his forties and had moved there from inner-city Dublin. He now commuted up and down a few days each week. 'It's another world here, I tell ya, another world.' Looking out over the sparkling sea, I could certainly appreciate his sentiment.

The village of Dunmore East looked idyllic beside its boat-filled bay as I made my way down the hill to grab some food and catch up on some blogging before heading back to camp. I decided I'd better meet my hosts before it got too late – meeting a strange hitchhiker in sunlight was undoubtedly much better than meeting one in darkness.

Arriving back at the field, I sheepishly approached a group of people who were preparing food around a fire while their children ran free, using up the last of their energy before bedtime. 'Hey, you must be Ruairí!' one of the group called out. 'Joe told us about ya! Come on over, have a cuppa with us and tell us about this trip you're on.' Before long, I was back in my element, chatting with my new friends about the meaning of life before the topic turned to campfire ghost stories that possibly spooked me more than they did the children.

Three couples and their children were staying at this improvised campsite. Some lived nearby, while others were visiting from farther afield. One woman was taking time out from her high-pressure media career, a few were teachers and one worked by night as a chef.

'Our summer camping adventure is something we started doing a few years ago,' said one of the women. 'It's great for the kids. They can run wild, and we don't have to worry about them. They get to be in nature, and we all get to share cooking and childcare responsibilities. We come and go sometimes, depending on the weather.'

'Excuse me, mister, would you like a footbath?' came a child's voice from behind me as I sat taking it all in.

'It's our nighttime foot spa ritual,' his mother added, explaining that the kids collected seaweed during the day and added it to basins of hot water each night. 'We all do it before bed, it's very relaxing.' Just as I had thought the day couldn't get any better. *Who knew such luxury was possible in a small field in the south of Ireland?* I thought to myself as I slipped my feet into the warm bath. So much for 'roughing it'. This was the life.

We sat around the campfire for another few hours, sharing stories and songs, before I decided to call it a night. Lying back in the wagon, I peeked out through the small window and watched the last of the fire's flames sending sparks into the starry night sky. *Is this the way we're meant to be living?* I wondered. Had the Travelling people who owned the wagon lived like this once? I imagined them moving from place to place in their tight-knit communities, offering their skills as tinsmiths, musicians and storytellers.

These days, such a lifestyle may not seem realistic. But is our new way of life really more civilised? We sit in traffic, stare at screens for hours on end and slave over an endless number of tasks so we can buy new devices that are supposed to make our lives simpler?

The mass introduction of plastic killed off the demand for tinsmiths, while a State policy of assimilation pushed the Travellers to give up their ways and settle down like 'the rest of us', leaving many to mourn their culture's demise while pushing them into reservation-style halting sites lacking basic facilities.

What happened to the people who had once owned the wagon I was sleeping in? Had they continued to travel the land, or did they end up living as settled Travellers in a town or city? I wondered if they were happy, or if they experienced the higher rates of unemployment, imprisonment and depression that their people often faced in a country where the life expectancy for Travellers is ten years lower than the national average and the suicide rate six times higher.*

'Get along, move along, get along, move along . . .' floated through my head, the words to a Ewan MacColl song that described the plight of Travellers continually forced to move on. It was a reminder of the prejudice that the Traveller people, or Mincéir people as they are known in their Cant language, have faced over the years. I knew I was overly romanticising things, but lying in the wagon that night, I couldn't help but think that perhaps there was something in those Traveller traditions – the communal life on the road and in the great outdoors – something that we could learn from amid the constant rush and push of the modern world.

* 'Gypsies and Travellers: Simple Solutions for Living Together,' Equality and Human Rights Commission, last updated October 23, 2017, https://www .equalityhumanrights.com/en/gypsies-and-travellers-simple-solutions -living-together; Sarah Stack, 'Traveller Suicide Rates Soar at Six-Times the Settled Community Numbers,' *Irish Independent*, October 4, 2011, https:// www.independent.ie/irish-news/traveller-suicide-rates-soar-at-sixtimes -the-settled-community-numbers-26778591.html.

13

Pain and Perspective

Dungarvan to Cork

THE CLOCK WAS TICKING DOWN TOWARDS THE DATE of my talk at the MacGill summer school in Donegal, and nearer to a decision that had to be made: Did I want to stick things out in Ireland or take the idea of emigration seriously? Amid the country's problems, I could understand why so many were leaving. At the same time, the trip was inspiring me and reawakening a fire that had needed some fuel. These questions would have to wait a little longer – for now I needed to focus on the road ahead.

'Lismore is amazing, as is Ring, an Irish-speaking area of about 500 people,' said a friendly local woman, distracting me from my contemplation when she picked me up just three minutes after Joe dropped me back on the main road. 'They are both worth checking out.' I had no idea there was an Irish-speaking Gaeltacht area around here. With the exception of Ráth Chairn in County Meath, where about 400 native Irish speakers live, and an emerging urban Gaeltacht in West Belfast, all the remaining Gaeltacht areas are dotted around the west coast, where they are on life support against the forces of anglicisation.

'If I were you, I'd definitely give Lismore a look,' she repeated before dropping me off at the edge of the N72 road just outside Dungarvan.

The day had started out well, but an hour later, I was still standing in the sweltering heat without water on a busy road, cars speeding by. It's never that practical to hitch on a busy road, as cars tend to be going too fast to slow down in time. I was beginning to think I should change direction when suddenly a man in a white van pulled over to offer me a lift. 'I'm only going up the road,' he said in a soft voice, 'but I can drop you at the next junction.'

He was on his way to an event at a local community forest. 'I've been involved with the project for a while now as a volunteer,' he explained. 'I just feel passionate about trees and reforestation. Did you know Ireland has the lowest rate of forest cover in Europe, despite having some of the best conditions for growing trees on the entire planet? The country was once covered in trees, but most were chopped down to make way for farmland and to build boats for the British Empire. Since then, successive governments have failed to implement a proper forestry policy. There's very little native woodland left. Most of our forestry is commercial, which isn't good for biodiversity.

'What we need is a real vision for forestry, especially for community woodlands. It's like the government and the EU want us to become one giant Christmas tree farm. They've even been talking about privatising what little forestry we do have. I think Bertie Ahern is involved in that. He's involved with some foreign fund that buys up forestry. Imagine that, the former leader of the country, working with foreign investors to try to buy the nation's forests! The Woodland League and others have a campaign against that, so hopefully we'll be able to stop it. Anyway, it's also important to get out there and enjoy the woodlands that we do have, and to plant new ones where we can, especially in the era of climate change. Events like today are great for doing that, and there's always a great atmosphere.'

I had some idea of what he was talking about. Several years before I had joined a successful campaign in my hometown to stop the State forestry company, Coillte, from cutting down some of the last remaining old-growth oaks. It was a small but convincing victory that mobilised hundreds of people, reminding us – and the powers that be – that some things are more important than money. What made the victory extra sweet was the fact that my friend Sem was able to attend the victory walk, sharing a traditional Papuan ceremony and a song in honour of the trees. From the jungles of Papua to the forests of Cootehill – it was a cultural fusion I will always cherish, and another example of people-power winning against the odds.

'I'll drop you off here, if you don't mind,' said the Cork man as we bid farewell.

Soon enough, a red rental car pulled over, and I jumped in to meet two young Swiss tourists. 'We're going to Cork City. What about you?' asked the fair-haired driver. 'I'm going there, too,' I replied, without too much hesitation. A direct lift was too good to resist. Lismore and Ring would have to wait for another day.

The Swiss guys were both on a break from stressful banking jobs. 'We love it here,' the driver continued. 'The pace of life is great. The police don't even carry guns. We've been out every night and the pubs are excellent.'

'So are the ladies!' his friend added from the passenger seat.

———

An hour later I said goodbye to the Swiss lads in the middle of Cork. The streets were alive with excitement for the World Street Performance Festival, which featured acrobats, dancers, stilt walkers and performers entertaining the public with their creative and comedic feats. I figured I would find a quiet spot but barely got 20 metres down the street before I bumped into Ken, a guy I knew from Dublin.

'Do you fancy a pint?' Ken asked with a mischievous glint in his eye. At the Roundy pub we were joined by my friend Damien, and the drinks and conversation flowed as we sat outside in the evening sun, mixing with a fun-loving crowd.

I figured I'd need accommodation soon. A guy named Kurt had been in touch on social media to offer his bedroom while he was abroad. He was involved in community work, including the Love Music Hate Racism campaign, but we had never actually met. I texted Kurt's house-mate to ask about the prospect of staying. Before long she arrived to join our growing motley crew as we relaxed into the evening sharing stories, jokes and smiles.

The next morning, I didn't feel quite so good, though I hadn't had much to drink. My tolerance had nosedived in recent years – just a few drinks would leave me curled up feeling sorry for myself. I'd had more than my fair share of crazy nights out over the years, but more recently hated losing the next day to sickness and regret. Increasingly, hangovers had begun to feel like a real waste of time when there was so much I wanted to accomplish.

I had also started to question people's relationship with alcohol in Ireland, where it seemed an accepted rite of passage to start drinking around the age of 15, sometimes even younger. Alcohol had adversely affected my family in various ways, as it does many Irish families. It didn't do any favours for my father in the past, nor for his father before him, and I have had plenty of run-ins with it too.

My major negative experience with alcohol happened when I was 19 years old. I was working in a stressful job for a multinational company in Scotland for a year as part of my university degree, offsetting the pressures by partying hard at night with my fellow students. Binge drinking was normal for most of my peers. We would dive into beer, cider and spirits in order to 'get out of our heads' as cheaply and quickly as possible. The results of this lifestyle all came to a head one day. I was sitting at my desk at work, feeling miserable from the effects of a big night out after watching the Celtic versus Rangers derby.

'You're looking very pale. Are you okay?' my colleague enquired, looking concerned. I went to the bathroom and looked in the mirror. I wasn't just pale; I looked grey, and my lips were cracked and colourless. I struggled through the day. But later, as I was leaving the building, I collapsed unconscious on the floor. I awoke seconds later to find myself dazed and drooling while someone strapped me into a wheelchair and pushed me through the crowds of workers heading out after work. It was not my finest hour.

The company nurse sent me home to rest. After several days in bed, my flatmate encouraged me to seek medical attention. I worked up the energy to take the five-minute walk to the doctor's surgery, where they immediately called an ambulance.

I was placed in a hospital ward full of elderly men and told I had lost a huge amount of blood due to a perforated stomach ulcer. I had experienced stomach pains since childhood. A degree of anxiety had a role to play, I'm sure, but alcohol abuse and a poor diet of convenience foods tipped the problem over the edge.

The experience was a major wake-up call. It forced me to the point where I hardly drink at all. My work over the years also prompted me to reflect on the role alcohol plays in Irish society, how it diminishes our potential as individuals and as a nation, and to what extent it is used as self-medication by people suffering from invisible wounds.

Reflecting on all of this, I decided to stay in bed for the morning. Kurt had kindly said I could stay another night, so I was in no hurry. I used the time to check my emails and found one from my friend Barry. 'McKiernan, you're not going to believe it,' he started. 'Apparently, there's a priest somewhere in Cavan that was talking about your hitching trip from the altar at mass this morning. He's using it to talk about Jesus and hope or something. Can you believe it? Saint McKiernan, my ass. If only he knew some of the stories I know!'

The message brought a broad smile to my face. That the trip was reaching people in person, through the media, and now through a religious service, was a sign that people were hungry for a different way of looking at things. And while I may have been the protagonist, the story was much bigger than me – it was opening up the story of Ireland, the story of issues affecting us on a global level. It was opening up a conversation about hope. It seemed, in that moment, that I was achieving something, modest and intangible perhaps, but significant all the same.

It was perhaps no accident that I was thinking about all of this on a quiet Sunday morning. The slowness and quietness of Sundays had often bothered me, challenging my constant impulse to be busy and productive. No wonder I had been prone to burnout. Increasingly, I was thinking of Sunday as a kind of sacred Sabbath, religion aside. It is essential to have a space for friends, family, rest and renewal – a chance for the spirit to catch up with the body during busy times.

———

Eventually, I dragged myself out of bed and retraced my steps into the city. I wandered past the street performers and tourists, through mural-filled back streets, and along the River Lee, which weaves through Cork's historic thoroughfares.

In the late afternoon, I stood outside the English Market looking at my phone for directions when a woman approached me. 'Excuse me, sorry to bother you, but are you the hitchhiker guy?' she asked, as her friend looked on, giggling, from across the street. 'We saw you on the TV the other day, and I think what you're doing is great.'

Sarah was in her thirties, and like many people her age who had stable work, she had taken out a 100 per cent mortgage. Because of the crash, the home she had bought was now worth only a fraction of its original price.

Her partner was self-employed, his work had dried up and he wasn't entitled to State support, meaning they were under severe financial pressure. Childcare costs were a huge burden, and the situation had contributed to the depression she had suffered over the past year.

'Politicians have forgotten about people like me,' she said in a tone markedly different from her initial greeting. I was taken aback. This woman had appeared out of nowhere to share her most private pain with me. I felt privileged that she would speak to me with such trust and honesty, and I felt for her.

'At the moment it's all doom and gloom, but you have to kind of keep your head up about it, you know? It does bring me down at times but I try to get out, go for a walk, go for a jog in the park, do my art and just try to be positive about things, because life is short and you have to make the most of it.'

Sarah seemed to have strong coping tools, but I thought once again of the many people who had internalised their suffering, believing it was the result of their own mistakes rather than part of a massive societal problem. Perhaps they saw themselves as failures, as I had myself at times. The system encourages that perception, leading people to suffer alone in silence, often medicated for depression. If only we could see the commonality of our struggles; if only we could see that it's not *we* who are broken, but the unhealthy system in which we live. As the Indian philosopher Krishnamurti once said, 'It is no measure of health to be well adjusted to a profoundly sick society.'

14

Fresh Perspectives

Cork to Limerick

I AWOKE THE NEXT MORNING TO A MESSAGE FROM MY friend Damien asking me if I'd like a lift to the outskirts of Cork – a welcome offer, as hitchhiking out of cities was always a challenge. 'Great! I'll pick you up at noon, and we'll go for lunch first,' he replied.

I knew Damien was a bit of a foodie, but I hadn't expected to end up in Fenn's Quay – a fancy restaurant that had received prestigious awards, including a Michelin recommendation. He introduced me to the owner and head chef, Kate Lawlor. When I asked about her experience of surviving in business, she said the recession, combined with high rents, commercial rates and a lack of support and understanding from the banks had been incredibly frustrating. But she was determined to keep going.

'I think the community needs to come together. It is, slowly but surely, using smaller producers, getting away from the big corporate companies if possible. In the next ten years, I would like to see Ireland flourishing. I would like to see more support for our type of business – small and local, rather than the big corporates.'

In so many places I'd visited so far, food and farming had emerged as significant issues. In a sugar-loving nation contending with an obesity crisis, I could only hope that this shifting focus on food would help reinstate the concept of food as medicine.

As we left Fenn's Quay, Damien shared his own thoughts on Ireland's rut. 'I think we need to disrupt everything,' he said. 'More people need to address the government directly. Tell them what we want. Insist on what we want and not let things go back to what is the default. We need to stop ending up in the same cycle; we have to change things around, change people around, bring in new thinking, try things and fail if needs be, but at least let's try things. We need to put people first and build around that.'

Damien dropped me at the side of the N20 to Limerick, suggesting that I start making my way northward to get to Donegal in the coming days. Soon after, the food theme continued during my lift with a Dutchman named Ron, who spoke passionately about his involvement with a local organic food buyers' group.

'What about the argument that organic food is just for the well off?' I challenged Ron.

'Well, you can say that,' he replied, 'but it's really about choices. Yes, there are cheaper vegetables and processed, packaged food in supermarkets, but what is their nutritional content? If you value the extra health benefits of organic food, not to mention the fact that they are better for the environment, then maybe it's worth paying a bit extra and cutting back on other things if you can. It's also possible to grow your own food – it just depends what you value.'

I had always admired the Netherlands and how they seem to have developed a well-functioning social democracy, so I was intrigued as to why Ron had chosen to live in Ireland.

'I came here because of a job offer, and when I visited the country to check it out, I loved the friendliness of the people and the wide-open spaces. Ireland has a lot going for it.'

Again, it was good to get the perspective of someone from elsewhere, helping me see what I often take for granted. Countries like the Netherlands, Germany and England are densely populated and heavily industrialised, whereas we still have a relatively clean and green landscape with plenty of space to roam.

As with many people I encountered, Ron said the major disappointment he had with Ireland was its lack of political vision and leadership.

'I think there's a post-colonial problem with Irish people not trusting the State, because for years the State was against them. My feeling is that people need to take ownership of the country and realise that they have to get involved in creating a national vision for Ireland. Politicians need to do more than represent their own local constituency so that we can further develop as a nation and create a better future for all.'

———

You never know what's coming next when you're hitching, and I certainly didn't expect my next lift to be from a man in a flashy sports car. Accepting the lift, I felt a bit uneasy. The driver wasn't as instantly warm and friendly as most. I was used to getting lifts with certain types of people in certain types of cars, and he didn't fit the bill. *Is this okay? Is this guy legit?* I wondered, imagining all sorts of scenarios. As always, I decided to go with my gut. It had served me well thus far.

It turned out the man was perfectly amenable. He was an accountant from France who had first come to Ireland on a family holiday over 20 years ago and found it 'wet and green, but very friendly', he recalled. He was 14 years old at the time.

'We arrived from the ferry in Rosslare, and it was really misty and wet. We got the train. It was hard to figure things out, and there was no information about times or destinations. People were so friendly, though. I remember looking for something to eat, and we asked a guy what to have and he told us to get fish and chips. It was my first time having this kind of food. Next thing the guy wanted to pay for our meal. We'd never experienced anything like that before.'

Curious, I asked him how he came to live here.

'I remember during that family holiday a moment when we were on the train, travelling close to the sea. The villages were lovely, and the weather was good. It was like Italy. People were open. It was then that I decided I wanted to live here. I now live in Limerick with my wife, who is also an immigrant to this country. I've heard some Irish people say there are no opportunities here, but we don't see it like that. There are so many opportunities if you open your mind. It's about attitude and how you perceive things.'

In another departure from much of what I had heard along the way, he remarked on Ireland's relatively stable political situation. 'There isn't so much of an internal fight going on here,' he pointed out. 'More and more of Europe is going in a fascist direction – in France, Austria and Germany there is huge unrest. Just yesterday in Paris the police shot some people. That doesn't tend happen here.

'The politics could be much better here, though. It's not as bad as elsewhere, but politics should be for the people. Too many politicians think about themselves, not the people. Ireland has gone from very poor to rich, especially with the advent of new technology. When I first came here, it was one of the poorest countries in Europe. Now, it's important to invest in education. That is the way to build a better future for the country.'

He mentioned the significance of travel in broadening people's horizons. 'When I was young, there were exchanges to bring young people together. Now, you have more and more nationalists who want to keep people apart. Europe should be a strong continent, but we must work together. We shouldn't forget our own culture and identity, but we need to come together. When you travel around, you get to know people – you see what we have in common, you realise that we have the same jokes, the same needs. There is no place then for nationalism and fascism.

'Life can give you good times,' he continued, 'but you have to get out, travel around, have an open mind and go beyond your own borders – the borders of your own country and those inside your head. This way, you become a better person.'

———

'Are you hungry? Would you like to join us for dinner?' my new friend asked after we parked up outside his house in the suburbs of Limerick. I couldn't lie: my stomach was rumbling, and it felt good to be welcomed into yet another home.

'I love it here, but it's hard at work,' his wife told me as we tucked into a yummy stew. 'My boss is not good and doesn't treat us right. Most of us are from Eastern Europe, and he messes us around with hours and pay, and talks down to us.' She said she had come across other instances of employers taking advantage of non-unionised immigrant workers who often don't know their rights or are too afraid to stand up for them.

'It's hard, but I have to stay strong,' she told me, explaining that she had recently started an evening course she hoped would build her skills and help her find better work. She had a determination and work ethic I'd noticed among immigrant communities the world over, including the Irish abroad. Immigrants often don't have the social networks, access or influence of native-born people, and might also have language and cultural barriers to overcome. Contrary to negative claims about immigrants on welfare, I had always found them to be entrepreneurial, resourceful and eager to succeed.

'I'm lucky,' she concluded. 'In Ireland there are a lot of opportunities for training and further education through evening courses. This way, no matter who you are, you can try to develop yourself.'

———

'Our place is a lot different from Glenstal, as you'll see shortly,' Jennifer explained as she picked me up at the grounds of the well-known Catholic monastery and private boarding school the next morning. Glenstal Abbey was on the outskirts of Limerick. I had stayed in their guesthouse the previous night after paying a surprise visit to my mother, who was on retreat there.

'Are you sure you don't want to check in here and give the monastic life a go, Ruairí?' my mother asked in jest as I set off for Limerick with Jennifer. Jennifer was the manager of the Learning Hub, a centre that worked with young people, especially those affected by poverty, unemployment and violence. She had contacted me on Twitter and was now bringing me to visit her workplace in Limerick.

'I've no problem with Glenstal specifically. I've heard it's an excellent school. But I do think we need to question why the State is sponsoring private schools like that through general taxation, especially when we have such levels of educational inequality in places like Limerick,' Jennifer said as we made our way into the city.

Arriving at the building where Jennifer worked, I noticed that the surrounding area was a sea of concrete, a stark contrast with the forested natural surrounds of Glenstal Abbey. The inside, however, was different – a high-energy festival of colour and activity.

'There's a big emphasis here on creativity, and on music, song, poetry and art,' a young volunteer told me. 'This place is about anything that helps people get their voices heard so they can express themselves. When this happens, people can really blossom. The opposite of this is when people bottle things up and don't express their emotions. That's why hip-hop has a particular appeal. It's about cultivating expression and confidence, and taking action. Action breeds hope,' she proclaimed.

Action breeds hope – that was a great mantra.

A musician who was listening in on our conversation expanded upon this sentiment: 'I think that in order to get the country going we need people taking responsibility for their actions, both the positive and the negative. That means individuals, rather than waiting for things to happen, have to seize whatever opportunities they can and actually make things happen, actually creatively stand up and do things.'

'We need to recognise,' he continued, 'the wrongs that we've done in the past and where it is appropriate to pursue those who have done wrong in the past, rather than sitting back and accepting that that's the way things are. We need to take our country back and lead from the bottom up and the top down.'

I thanked Jennifer and team at the Learning Hub and soon after met up with Allen, the editor of the Moyross-based *Changing Ireland* magazine. Jennifer had informed him I was in the area, and he offered to bring me on a tour of nearby Moyross, Ireland's largest social housing estate. Once home to over 4,000 people, Moyross was recovering from years of deprivation, crime, violence and neglect.

'When you look at an area like this, you have to put it all into context,' Allen explained. 'I know things are changing, but I remember reading a study that showed there were more golf courses than public playgrounds in Ireland at one point. There are more people in prison for minor offences than for the wholesale robbery of the nation. What does that tell you about power and priorities? We need to find a way of channelling our anger. We could change things in the morning if we did that,' he said with fire.

'Thankfully, regeneration efforts are paying off, and things are starting to change around here,' Allen continued as we walked around the vast estate surveying burned-out buildings and large green areas with horses that were used for sulky cart racing.

Being in Moyross reminded me of the stories my father Seán had told me about growing up in a council house in Cavan town. I had spent much of my own childhood there with my grandmother Maisie, who looked after me while my parents were at work. While Maisie provided a loving home for my father and his siblings, he said those living in council houses sometimes encountered stigma and prejudice that could have lasting effects. 'As council tenants, we weren't allowed to borrow books from the library the same way other people could. We had to have a signed guarantor as security. Those experiences are part of the reason I do the work that I do,' he once told me, explaining his decision to work with young people on the margins of society.

'You know, we have a lot to be grateful for,' Allen said, shaking me from my thoughts. 'Look at Ireland in the global context: when you look at so many other countries around the planet, we're still part of a rich minority of sorts. It's all relative, but either way, inequality is something that is screaming out for our attention,' he concluded before dropping me off on a country road on the outskirts of Limerick.

My mind spun with thoughts of class, separation and segregation as I stood waiting on a lift to take me north into County Clare. At a time when the very future of our planet hangs in the balance, what hope do we have if we continue to foster divisions based on class, race, religion and gender? Still, much of what I had heard that morning proved that there were so many heroes out there making change happen. As the volunteer at the Learning Hub had so eloquently reminded me: action breeds hope.

15

Community Healing

Killaloe

THERE'S SOMETHING MAGICAL ABOUT KILLALOE. THE
small town in County Clare sits at the base of Lough Derg, hugged
by hilly forests that conceal it from the outside world. The village of
Ballina lies right across a stunning, 300-year-old, 13-arch bridge that
marks the border with County Tipperary.

This was the final phase: a quick overnight in Killaloe and then a
push through the middle of the island to County Donegal in the northwest. The only problem was, I didn't want the trip to end. I was just
hitting my stride, doing the things I love most: travelling, listening to
people, helping them share their stories, engaging with the media, and
hopefully helping to spread ripples of change.

Arriving into Killaloe, I instantly relaxed. The quiet streets and
gently flowing river oozed an air of tranquillity. It was getting late,
and unusually for this trip, no obvious accommodation options had yet
emerged. I felt a natural push towards getting a bed and breakfast for
the night – a chance for my introverted side to enjoy a little solitude.

The next morning, I ventured out onto the streets of Killaloe and before long found myself peeking through the window of the Killaloe/Ballina Community & Family Resource Centre, the front area of which looked like a café. I walked in, ordered a coffee, and sat down to watch and listen. Beside me, two men were deep in discussion about some kind of social project they were involved in. To their left was a young mother feeding her baby, and behind them an older woman was consoling another who looked like she had been crying. The place was small, clean and simple, the walls covered in bright posters and artwork. The chatty volunteers seemed to know everyone by name.

Eventually I decided to introduce myself and risk the 'is this guy for real?' reaction. My apprehension was rooted more in fear than in reality; at almost every stage of the trip, I had found people approachable, helpful, and immediately open to what I was doing. I could feel the kindness gradually restoring the part of myself that used to be more open, confident and trusting.

Within minutes of saying hello, I was being whisked around to meet everyone before being led on a lively tour of the building. I learned about the 'men's shed' initiative, which creates spaces for men to gather, chat, learn and support each other. 'The shed helps ease loneliness, and it gives lads a place to share some of their troubles and connect with other men without any pressure on them,' said one of the men involved.

A young volunteer told me she had been through some hard times, but the resource centre had restored her confidence, for which she would be eternally grateful. She said she had first encountered the resource centre while completing a course there, but loved it so much she returned as a volunteer, with a particular passion for engaging and empowering young people.

'Young people need opportunities and ways to find their place in the world. They deserve support and to be pointed in the right direction, a chance to enjoy life and not to be slagged off in the media, just because they're wearing a hoodie or something. We've also got to do more for our LGBTQ+ community,' she said, explaining the challenges that come with limited public transportation and few safe spaces to socialise.

Outside in the sun-filled courtyard, I heard from Bróna, the centre's assistant manager. 'I want to see a country that wakes up. People feel disempowered and disengaged from politics, but whether we like it or not, it's still a structure that matters. We need to be challenging the people in power to think about the realities of family life for young people. There are a lot of people who feel they don't have a future here. They feel trapped, trapped by debt. You can create your own opportunities, but you need confidence and skills to do it,' she declared.

'One of the first places you can do that is through education. The State needs to step in, but instead, education budgets are being slashed. A lot of the labour activation initiatives around now aren't adventurous or dynamic enough. One of the big problems in Ireland is that we don't give ourselves room to innovate and fail. Everything has to work. Then what you find is that a lot of projects are funded long-term with core funding, and the State won't intervene when they're not working. Failure is a dirty word – but failure is how you try new things and find new solutions.'

Bróna's insight reflected a truth perhaps not unique to Ireland, but rather a condition of the global economic order. This system wasn't structured to allow wriggle room; it was built to ensure perpetual forward motion that shows little or no lenience towards those who face setbacks. Except, of course, for the banks, corporations and other big players who are often deemed too important to be left to fail.

'You have to keep the dream alive, Ruairí,' Bróna continued. 'I would love to see a more equal Ireland, with more equal living standards and access to health. I'd like to see a happier, healthier country, a more positive country,' she added hopefully.

Throughout my trip, I had frequently encountered this perception that the world is increasingly divided into the haves and the have-nots. As it happened, I was about to be introduced to a man who had lived on both sides of that divide. Ray was in his early seventies – a former corporate executive who had earned a lot of money and travelled the world, but in recent years had lost everything. His relationship with his family had become strained, and ill health had brought him to the brink of death.

'I need to head off now, but here's my address. Come around to my apartment tonight and I'll tell you more,' he said, looking me right in the eye before heading out the door.

———

'You have to interview Noreen. She's a star,' Bróna said with gusto. Noreen was the woman behind the counter who had served me when I first came in. She was in her late fifties, with bright red hair and glasses.

Noreen was reluctant to talk at first, but once she got going, there was no stopping her. She was insightful, witty, passionate and funny.

'The country is on its knees,' she declared. 'It's going nowhere. That's my honest opinion. I told my son to get back to New Zealand with his baby,' she said, joining the ranks of those whose lives were complicated by the emigration of loved ones.

'It makes me angry. When I was young, I had to leave too. I went to England. I had sisters who died there. I was the only one came back home. I always came back to my mother,' she said, before highlighting another recurring point. 'Life was simpler then. Kids today are preoccupied with computers and can't think for themselves. Years ago, people did their own cooking, sewing, baking, whitewashing their own houses. They could do their own things.'

Despite everything, Noreen also had a fierce sense of loyalty to the country that had so frustrated her: 'I love Ireland because it's who we are and because it's part of me. It's who I am, and I couldn't be happy anywhere else. I've always felt that,' she said, putting her hand to her heart.

'Why do you think the country is on its knees?' I probed, attempting again to peel back the veil that lay over some of Ireland's issues.

'Because the people are foolish,' she snapped. 'We're not standing up to the government. I just think we should get up and walk up there and say, "No more." If someone keeps slapping you on the face and you turn the other cheek for another belt, it'll keep happening.'

I wanted to know if Noreen, herself, was prepared to protest.

'Oh yes, I would. I would. I would go up to the Dáil if I could get someone to come with me. We need the people to start organising something so we can start marching up there.'

I was curious if Noreen had a sense of what kind of country she would like to see.

'A country where everyone is one, a country where you're not elected because of who your father or your grandfather was,' she replied. 'I want to see fresh faces, ordinary Joe Soaps who know what it's like for you and me and how we do things.'

Noreen looked more and more animated as she went on, so I pressed her for more. 'In the dark times, when people are struggling, where do you think hope comes from?'

'It comes from the people. From the local people giving hope to the local people. It has to start somewhere, and it starts in places like this,' she said with pride.

I asked her to tell me about the resource centre.

'I love it. When I came in here, I was very shy. I couldn't talk to anyone. I have learned to talk, to write, to work the computer, do finances, add up a couple of bob. I couldn't even do any of that. I mean, I was working at 14 years of age. So, it's great that I actually get the chance to do that now. And I think this is where the people need to grow from.'

Noreen was beaming. For a woman who had been shy, she had certainly found her voice. While some of her words came from a place of frustration and anger, she carried herself with warmth and integrity. It was voices like hers I wanted to hear and amplify – voices of people with stories to tell and fire in their bellies.

'I moved to Killaloe to prepare to die, in a way,' the former executive, Ray, said with solemnity when I visited him at his home later that evening. 'I got this one-bedroom apartment and hid myself away with my medication. I didn't see anyone except for the nurse who would check up on me occasionally. I had lost faith and was full of regret about how I had lived my life.' He had an air of sadness as we sat among a scattering of books and boxes of medication.

'I used to go for one daily walk, and over time found myself looking in the door of the resource centre, wondering what was going on in there. I didn't have the confidence nor the inclination to go inside. But I was curious. Eventually Noreen spotted me one day and called me inside for a cup of tea. The rest is history, as they say. Slowly but surely, my life began to turn around. I suppose I started to feel hope again. It all started with Noreen's invite and that cup of tea. In a way, her seeing me saved my life.'

Ray's voice trembled with emotion as he spoke. This was not a story he had shared with many people.

'In the centre I felt so welcomed and supported, part of a wider community. I started to visit every day, and when I didn't, someone would come looking for me. My health improved, and I started to get more involved in the centre by using some of my technology skills to create videos and run workshops to teach others. I felt I had a purpose again, something to believe in and contribute to.'

The corporate world had taught Ray a certain way of being, and he sometimes found himself fighting too hard for the control he was so accustomed to seeking.

'I would start to push for structure, and things like tangible targets, outcomes and outputs. I couldn't understand the flat structures in the resource centre, where people are seen as equal and everyone is involved. It just didn't make sense to me – it was a bit of a culture shock. I kept finding myself pushing for hierarchy, deadlines and linear progress, but each time I did, I'd be pushed back and told: "That's not the way we do things around here." Really, it's all more about the process than the finish line. It's frustrating, but it is starting to make sense. It's like learning a new language of how to be in the world. The biggest part of that is learning to slow down.'

As I thought about Ray and his new life, I considered the idea that personal transformation is like re-wiring yourself – unlearning and deprogramming what you've been taught over the years.

'It seems to me like you're already on that particular road,' he said as we bid each other good night.

———

The weather was balmy and the water perfectly still as I walked out by the boats moored up on the River Shannon. I had decided to walk towards the historic site of Brian Boru's fort, just down from Lough Derg, before heading to sleep, to let the evening's conversation sink in. Brian Boru was high king of Ireland from 1002 until his death at the Battle of Clontarf in 1014. This was where he developed the power base that helped him become one of Ireland's most successful and unifying medieval monarchs.

After a pleasant 20-minute stroll, a small, forested pathway brought me to the fort – a large mound of earth about 10 metres high and perhaps 70 metres wide. I looked down into a large flattened area of earth and imagined the ghosts of those who lived there over a millennium ago.

Just as my thoughts turned to the supernatural, I heard voices from the other side of the mound – they were men's voices, and they were growing louder. My initial fear turned to annoyance at whoever was back there spoiling my evening peace.

I figured it might be best to call it a night and avoid risking a confrontation. Then I realised how ridiculous that seemed – I was supposed to be exploring, meeting people, taking chances. So, I climbed up the eastern side of the fort and looked down. In the fading light, I spied a group of teenage guys who had set up camp.

'Howya, lads. My name is Ruairí. I'm travelling around Ireland and was just out for a walk when I heard you here. I hope you don't mind me coming over to say hello?' The lads looked at me, taking a few seconds to determine whether I was some kind of weirdo come to cause trouble.

'Not at all, come on over and tell us the craic,' said a tall, slim fella, while the others looked on with raised eyebrows and doubtful expressions. After I explained what I was up to, the remaining ice broke. 'Do you want something to eat or drink?' another asked, welcoming me into their royal domain.

'So, is the hitching hard then? Does it take long to get lifts?' His stocky, fair-haired friend wanted to know.

'Are ya meeting any axe murderers?' another joked as I settled in among them.

It turned out they were school pals on an overnight camping trip. 'We wanted to get out of the city – change of scene, you know? Beats all the shitty pubs and clubs in town, and it's cheaper!' one of the lads chipped in.

I sat for a while before asking about their plans for after they left school.

'I'll probably end up emigrating, but I don't want to because I love Ireland so much. I love our heritage, people, history, culture, everything,' said the red-haired guy to my right.

'I think we should leave this stuff to the politicians,' said his pal. 'It's their job. I can't vote, so I don't really see why I should care. Besides, we're preoccupied with other stuff.'

Another, who had lived in a few other countries already, had a different take. He appeared politicised and particularly passionate about the media. 'I don't trust the mainstream news. Basically, I get my news from the internet. I get it from the Reddit website and places like that. That American whistleblower guy, Edward Snowden – now, he's cool. He is the one guy who stands out from the crowd. He gave up his $200,000 salary to alert us to the government's bullshit, like you know, stealing our privacy and spying on us. You know the PRISM scheme that Snowden uncovered? Apparently even the Xbox is in on that. Snowden is seriously cool. He gave it all up to basically give us our freedom.'

'So, should Ireland offer sanctuary to Snowden?' I asked.

'Yeah. I think we kind of kiss America's ass, and I think letting Snowden in would kind of show that we can stand our ground and be independent.'

His friend wasn't so sure. 'I don't know. I wouldn't mind if he came to Ireland, but I think that would affect the American-Ireland relationship.'

It was heartening to see a group of young friends able to appreciate and consider each other's different perspectives. And it was refreshing to see them taking advantage of the outdoors. In a modern world where young people are too often forced to stay indoors, in fear of strangers, away from adventure and stuck before screens, there's a lot to be said for getting out into the sticks with your buddies, taking road trips and making memories.

It was getting dark by then. I thanked the guys for the beer and told them, with a serious face, to watch out for Brian Boru's ghost, saying I thought I had spotted it earlier.

'Ah yeah, nice one, man,' said one of the lads. His pals laughed before they all went silent for a second, as if thinking: *What if he's serious?*

———

Back at the bed and breakfast, I noticed a missed call and a voicemail on my phone.

'Hello, Ruairí. I'm calling from the Office of the President,' a woman informed me. 'The President has called a meeting of the Council of State, and we need to get in touch with you fairly urgently.'

It was almost midnight, but I decided to call back.

'Yes, it's all very short notice. The meeting is in a few days' time, and we need to get a box of documents to you urgently, so you have a chance to prepare.'

This news would change everything. I had no plan to return to Dublin, and I certainly hadn't envisaged spending the final days of my trip immersed in legislation. However, a Council of State meeting was a big deal, and I needed to treat it with due respect. The President only convenes these meetings in exceptional circumstances, to seek advice on the constitutionality of a piece of legislation before either signing it or referring it to the Supreme Court.

'Can you tell us the best address to deliver the box and I'll arrange a Garda to come over to you?' the woman wanted to know.

Oh dear. How could I answer this? I was due to hit the road again and had no idea where they might be able to reach me.

'Well, the thing is . . .' I said hesitantly, realising this was likely not a typical issue brought up by members of the Council of State, 'I'm on this hitchhiking trip, and I honestly don't know where I'll be tomorrow.'

16

The Heart of Ireland

Ballina to Uisneach

'HEY MCKIERNAN, I SEE MICHAEL D. HAS CALLED A Council of State meeting. You better quit your rambling and get your ass home pronto!' read one of the many messages on my phone the next morning.

It did seem that I would have to dramatically change course, especially once I had called the woman back to instruct her where to send the package.

'It's a pretty big box full of documents, and there's a lot of reading in it,' she remarked. 'There are several thousand pages – it's approximately the size of a microwave.' I tried to remain calm. The huge responsibility of what lay ahead was too important, meaning I could no longer go with the flow. It was abundantly clear that the box would be too much to travel with, and the subject matter too important to carry around lightly. In the end, we agreed it was best to send it to my local Garda station in Dublin.

I packed up and headed downstairs for what could well be my last breakfast of the trip. As I sat there sipping coffee among the other guests, the radio news came on and announced the news of the Council of State meeting. I could see people's ears perking up. Council of State meetings were rare, generally held only once every few years. *Oh dear,* I thought, trying to gather myself. *This is happening. I really need to get organised, and fast.*

Mild anxiety crept in. How would I prepare in time? What format would the meeting take? Would I have to debate or make a presentation? Most importantly, what about the issue: the Protection of Life During Pregnancy legislation, which was designed to legalise abortion in cases where pregnancy endangers a woman's life. This was the very same piece of legislation I had discussed with Janet and friends back in Letterkenny. What advice would I give the President on whether he should sign the bill or refer it to the Supreme Court? This wasn't a task to take lightly. I had a decent grasp of the issues and a core confidence, but unlike most of the other Council of State members, I was no lawyer, politician, academic or constitutional expert. Then again, I was appointed for a reason: I was a voice from the community and I needed to hold firm and honour this opportunity and the question at hand.

I sat and thought. I had five days until the meeting and would probably need at least three of those for reading and preparation. If I was focused and consulted some experts, I could probably swing at least another day or two on the road, making phone calls, reading, and reflecting on the issues as I went. I could wind things up with less panic if I left immediately to head up through the midlands, and after that straight home to Dublin.

Above all, I wanted to see if I could make it to a place that had been calling me, a very special place at the centre point of Ireland: the ancient Hill of Uisneach.

———

I headed across the river to the village of Ballina to find a good spot to start hitching. Today, every hour felt more precious than it had the day before.

Half an hour later, I was still there and starting to worry. Cars passed every couple of minutes but ignored me. This was not an opportune time for my luck to suddenly shift.

I took a break to get a cool drink in a nearby shop. However, the unease continued to mount when I spotted myself on the front page of a newspaper, in a group photo of the President's seven Council of State appointees. This was slightly surreal. So much for the initial intention of going on a low-key trip that I would only speak about at the end.

Returning to the road, I waited for another 20 minutes until finally a nervous-looking woman in her early thirties stopped. 'I saw you hitching earlier. I don't normally pick people up, but it seems like you've been here a long time, so I figured, why not?'

'I never pick up hitchhikers,' she repeated, and I did my best to assure her that she needn't worry. She was a social worker on her way to Nenagh to do a home visit. She told me about her job and the range of issues she encountered each day, including domestic violence and child abuse. *How does she do it?* I wondered.

'It's stressful, there's no doubt about that. But I love it, too. It's very rewarding, and it's what I want to be doing. The biggest challenge at the moment is that I'm on a short-term contract and it's hard to plan with that. You can't get a mortgage, buy a house or plan a life,' she said with a frustration I knew only too well.

Arriving into Nenagh, I thanked the woman for an eye-opening chat and walked towards the outskirts of town to hitch on. I considered making my way to Cloughjordan – a farming town with an adjoining ecovillage – to learn about their fascinating experiment in rural revival. From there I could go straight to Dublin. I thought about it for a while, but the pull of Uisneach was ultimately too strong.

I made my way in the sweltering heat towards the exit road to the northbound N52. My mind was still whirling with thoughts of the Council of State meeting. The proposed legislation, which had arisen partly in response to Savita Halappanavar's death during pregnancy, was highly controversial. It cut straight to the heart of the Irish nation, calling into question the influence of Catholicism on the State. The question as to whether the President should sign the legislation or refer it to the Supreme Court would surely heat up, and I was already receiving emails from campaigners seeking to influence my stance.

Deep in thought, I had almost forgotten my thumb was out when a silver car pulled over. 'I'm going as far as Borrisokane, if that suits?' said the driver, an older man wearing a priest's collar.

'People are too cautious these days that's for sure,' the priest said. 'They need to get out of their boxes a bit more, if you ask me.

'Can I ask, are you a Christian?' he eventually ventured. I had been hoping we weren't going to go there.

'Well, I was brought up Catholic,' I answered, attempting a diplomatic fudge before elaborating a little. 'I'm not a practicing Catholic anymore. I have my own set of beliefs, my own spirituality, but I also agree with a lot of what are considered Christian values,' I added, aiming for middle ground.

'Well, Jesus is your only man, I can tell you that now. If you follow him, you'll be alright,' he replied. I could see where he was coming from and had no real argument – Jesus was big on spreading love and justice in the world, and indeed, on challenging authority – things the world certainly needs more of – but I believe there have been many other prophets, teachers and healers worth taking inspiration from.

By the time we arrived in Borris, as it's known locally, I was enjoying the elderly priest's company and didn't want to part ways. He was the oldest person to have given me a lift so far – in his eighties, he told me. Rather than sit back into a quiet retirement, he spent his days visiting sick people and helping those who were dying – a man walking his talk.

———

Standing on the street in Borrisokane, I felt as if I had stepped back in time. Tractors drove up and down a relatively empty main street flanked by boarded-up buildings and fading shop signs that whispered of an age gone by. A few older folk hobbled along, perhaps looking for company in a recession-hit town that many had clearly departed.

Distracted by the rumbling of my stomach, I went into a traditional-looking pub, where I sat in the corner and nodded to the only other customers – an elderly couple watching the news.

On the wall was a photograph of actor Martin Sheen, who, it seemed, had visited the pub. I recalled that Sheen's mother, Mary-Anne Fieland, was from Borrisokane and that he held an Irish passport. I had seen him on the news back in 2003 when, while playing US President Bartlet on the hit TV show *The West Wing*, he had given a symbolic presidential pardon to a real-life group called the Pitstop Ploughshares, who were on trial in Ireland for an anti-war protest at Shannon Airport.

'I see Lowry is in trouble again,' the bartender said to me as she took my plate. The television was showing a news report about former government minister Michael Lowry, now an independent member of Dáil Éireann. He had been embroiled in various controversies before, and now the authorities had raided his home and seized files and documents. 'It's hard to see if anything will happen. It rarely does,' she said, with an air of resignation.

The day was flying by, and it was now close to three in the afternoon. I needed to keep moving if I was to reach Uisneach. Standing with my thumb out on the edge of town, a large black car seemed to appear out of nowhere.

'Hop in,' said the shaven-headed driver. There was something about this guy that unnerved me a bit. It was one of those moments where you have seconds to rely on your instinct and intuition before you make a decision.

'Come on, hop in,' he said again, and I obliged. He revved up and sped off, curving around the narrow roads at an unsettling speed that left me somewhat queasy after my lunch. 'Where are ya going?' he wanted to know.

'Uisneach, out past Mullingar.'

'Perfect, I'm going to Mullingar, so I can drop ya there,' he offered, his strong midlands accent coming through.

'Hitching for hope? Fair play to ya,' the man said when I told him about my journey. 'It's important to spread the positivity, you know, to do good stuff. I'm always doing charity events and raising money for local causes. I don't have as much time as I used to, as I have the kids, but I do my best.'

I started to realise that my first impression of the man was off – this guy was a softie with a big heart. The shaven head and fast car had thrown me. I had judged him as soon as I saw him, falling into a trap that I'm always encouraging others to avoid. I suppose it's part of being human; we need to process things quickly and sometimes come to the wrong conclusions. Still, it was a good kick in the ass for me.

'I'll tell you what, I'll drop you at the turn-off, and you'll be all sorted for a handy spin out to Uisneach,' he said, cementing his kindness by going out of his way to help me.

Uisneach was now just a short trip away. A warm breeze blew over me as I contemplated this last evening of hitching with a flicker of sadness. I didn't want this magic to end – to return to my so-called normal life. I wanted to maintain this sense of possibility, living a life of freedom and flow.

As I stood there with my thumb up, the phone rang. An editor with the *Irish Independent* wanted me to write an article about the journey – by the next day. I wasn't sure how I'd fit it in, but I figured it was a timely opportunity to share a summary of my insights and reflections as I made my way back to Dublin, so I agreed. First, though, I needed to get to Uisneach and perhaps set up camp there for the night.

A lift arrived minutes later – a local woman on her way home who offered to drop me at Killane, a 25-minute walk from the hill. I asked her about the protest posters I observed dotting the roadside as we drove along. 'Oh, they're about the turbines,' she replied. 'There's big plans to put giant skyscraper-size wind turbines in this area, and there's huge opposition. A few of us have got together and studied it all, and there are definite issues around the impact these turbines have on human health, not to mention wildlife and the landscape. There's hard evidence out there on this. It's not that we're against development or jobs, or any of that. God knows we need green energy, but this isn't the way to go. We just want to see sensible development, but it has to be done in partnership with the community, not the usual railroading that goes on. That's why there's so much opposition. I'll tell you what, we're not going down without a fight.'

The roads were quiet as I walked towards Uisneach, aside from the birds singing their contentment after another day in the sun. Turning a corner, I got my first glimpse of the hill. Standing at just 182 metres, Uisneach is somewhat hidden. It wasn't as if I was approaching the summit of Everest, but it was somehow exciting that a place of such significance could sit there in relative secrecy.

At the entrance stood a sign: 'Welcome to Uisneach – site of Celtic festival of Bealtaine, ancient place of assembly, St. Patrick's Church, sacred centre of Ireland in pagan times, site of druidic fire cult, seat of high kings.'

Uisneach is privately owned, part of a working farm. The owners, David and Angela Clarke, are passionate about returning Uisneach to the national consciousness and have worked tirelessly to open it up to the community as well as to the many archaeologists, historians, academics and mythologists who visit from all over the world.

I had been to the hill before and attended events connected with Bealtaine, the ancient fire festival that marks the start of summer. While on the surface there are no obvious temples or ruins, the more you explore the hill, the more you realise the vast wealth of treasures it holds in trust for those who care to look deeper.

To the right of the entrance sign was a house, where a notice on the gate requested visitors to phone for permission to continue. After a quick call to David Clarke, I proceeded upwards with all the excitement of a scout on a great adventure.

The hill is divided into a series of fields separated by fences and hedges, and home to hundreds of cows. Several years earlier, on my first visit to Uisneach with my friend Cormac, we'd engaged in a strange showdown with cows that emerged from all directions, lining up and blocking us from proceeding to the top. We stood there, looking at each other, thinking: *Is this for real?* Eventually we realised we wouldn't be able to face ourselves if we were run off the hill by a herd of cows. We walked slowly towards them in a tense standoff that lasted only until we reached them. At that moment, the row of cows parted as if in a welcoming ritual. The memory of us standing there in disbelief still makes me laugh.

Evening was setting in on the hill, and it felt like the perfect culmination of this trip to camp out alone and reflect. This was, after all, the heart of the island – a place once known as its fifth province, a sacred spiritual and political point keeping watch over the others.

The sky had begun to darken, and clouds were threatening rain on what minutes ago had appeared a calm summer evening. I walked to the very top of the hill, to a site known as St. Patrick's Bed, where a concrete and copper triangulation point marks the supposed centre of Ireland. It's said that on a clear day, it is possible to see up to 20 of Ireland's 32 counties from this point.

I was awash with emotions. Gratitude, excitement, nervousness and sadness all bubbled within me as I stood there, surveying the horizon, taking in the great expanse of this hill of magic and memory. Within 24 hours I would be at home in Dublin preparing for a very different experience. But this experience felt just as important, and was perhaps all part of the preparation. The clouds were growing darker by the minute, and I hurried to pitch my tent before running down to the southwest slope, over a fence and into a field full of cows. I wanted to get to the jewel of Uisneach, Aill na Mireann ('the stone of divisions') – a sacred, fragmenting limestone boulder said to mark the spot where the borders of the ancient provinces met and the burial place of the mythical goddess Ériu, after whom Ireland is named. Its nickname, the Catstone, reflects a more light-hearted resemblance: the stone looks to some like a cat watching a mouse.

Raindrops began to fall as I approached the towering rock, which stands six metres tall and is made up of two giant boulders with a cave-like passage beneath them. A breeze blew as I started to climb up the rock to the highest level. I found my balance at the top and stood there with arms stretched out wide in triumph and joy.

Cultures the world over have a tradition of honouring the four directions, and there seemed no better place than on top of Ériu to give a nod to the north, south, east and west, as well as to what some traditions call 'Mother Earth' and 'Father Sky'. As I turned, I thought of the four provinces of Ulster, Munster, Leinster, and Connaught. I thought of the people in these lands, those who were suffering, downtrodden and in need of hope. I recalled all those I had met, the many people doing amazing things and holding torches of truth and transformation aloft. I reflected on all that this island had been through – the wars, violence, abuses – and what the future might bring. Then, with a deep breath, I sent a wish in each direction, that people might find whatever healing they needed and the courage to claim their power.

As I stood in this place of solitude, time seemed somehow to stand still. Rather than regard the rain as an enemy and run for cover as I would usually do, I stood there and loved it. I felt free from the pressure of what people might think of me. My thoughts folded into a dream-like state, where the past and future seemed to disappear. There was only the here and now, the raw richness of the moment and the elements surrounding me. I began to transcend all thought, fear, worry and doubt, connecting with what felt like an ancient sense of spirit. I felt simultaneously tuned into a deeper space within myself and into the particular power of this place, the force of which rippled through my body.

I felt a sudden urge to let out a shout of joy, and just as I did, the heavens opened, and the rain came hammering down. The cows looked up, perhaps wondering why a strange wild man was bellowing from atop a rock.

'Yes!' I shouted out into the rain, stretching my arms to the world.

17

The Royal Road Home

Uisneach to the Hill of Tara

I AWOKE SUDDENLY, BLEARY-EYED AND BURSTING TO use the toilet as I tried to remember exactly where I was. A dawn chorus of birdsong, cow moos and snores from the tents beside me filled the air like the choir in a natural cathedral. I stumbled out of the sleeping bag into the morning dew and walked barefoot to relieve myself in a ditch.

I had managed only about three or four hours' sleep, and struggled to open my eyes. Looking into the distance, I was suddenly captivated. The sun was starting to rise over distant hills, and I was spellbound as it illuminated the land around me. Enthralled, I watched the sun edge upwards and fill the sky with its radiance. *If only I could start every day like this*, I thought.

The sun triggered something primal in me, offering a reminder that I was part of a bigger story – a living, breathing cosmos; the delicate, interwoven fabric of life. It seemed obvious, in that moment, why our ancestors had worshipped the sun as the ultimate source of life, and why the solstices were such significant markers in the annual calendar. Here on Uisneach, I felt the undercurrent of an ancient story begging to be remembered.

'McKiernan, what are ya doing up so feckin' early, man?' Eoin shouted from his tent a few metres back, snapping me out of my musings. Two friends, Eoin and Martin, had arrived from my hometown of Cootehill just as night fell the previous evening. Eoin had seen on social media that I was heading to Uisneach and texted me as I returned from the Catstone to dry off in my tent.

My initial impulse was to ignore the message. He wanted to come and spend the night, but I felt this should be a solo adventure – a time to be alone with my thoughts and prepare for the return to Dublin and whatever came next. However, another voice in my head cut in. 'Don't be such a dull bore,' it taunted. I was blissfully happy on the hill on my own, enjoying the silence, but I knew I had a tendency to be too reclusive at times. I was always going on about the importance of community, but I'd often find ways of avoiding people and retreating into my shell. Here was an opportunity to share a special time with some good men from my hometown, to lighten up and have a bit of a laugh. Taking on the world's troubles can take its toll, and if there was one thing I needed more of, it was fun.

I had just enough power left on my phone to call Eoin and tell him to come over. 'We'll be up in about an hour and a half,' came the enthusiastic reply. 'We're good to go. We've lots of grub and fuel for a fire. It'll be mighty.'

As soon as I hung up, I realised I had no food. My trip certainly had a way of delivering what I needed just in time. This time, food was on its way before I even knew it was missing.

'Yeow!' Eoin shouted excitedly as he came into sight down the hill. I couldn't help but smile; this was going to be a good night. It didn't take long for them to set up camp, and we soon had a fire burning and food cooking. The chats and the laughs meant a lot to me, and I could see the lads were loving it, too.

Eoin had recently lost his dad, Pete, who was a local legend around Counties Cavan and Monaghan. After that, Eoin travelled the world and became interested in the indigenous cultures of Colombia, Australia and New Zealand, which in turn inspired him to learn more about our own native Irish traditions. Martin's mother had died in recent years. He had worked in architecture during the boom but lost his job when the construction industry collapsed. Unlike many of his peers, he had stuck it out in Cavan, preferring not to emigrate, while he explored new opportunities.

There was something healing about sitting around the fire, joking and laughing, watching the evening sky transform into a star-filled canvas. Therapy comes in many forms – music, art, walking, writing and counselling – but it's hard to beat the power of good company, a type of soul medicine no doctor or drug can provide. That the visit from Eoin and Martin was entirely unplanned made it all the more sweet.

'What the hell is that?' Eoin asked, pointing to a light at the top of the hill. We looked up, confused.

The light was coming from some kind of structure, but I had no idea what. It made no sense for somebody to be roaming around on the hill at this late hour. We looked closer. We could see what looked like two silhouettes walking around.

'Maybe it's the ghosts of Uisneach coming to say hello,' Eoin joked. It was as if my teasing back at Brian Boru's fort in Killaloe was coming back to haunt me, literally. I decided to investigate.

'If I'm not back in 20 minutes or you hear screaming, come and find me!' I joked. I grabbed a torch and walked up the hill, to where the outline of a dome became visible. I got closer and realised it was a yurt, with people moving around inside. Whoever they were, they were our neighbours for the night, so I decided to introduce myself.

A smiling, grey-haired man with sparkling eyes came bouncing out, as if he had somehow been expecting me. 'Ah Jasus, howya? What's the craic?' he asked, and introduced himself as Marty. 'Come on inside. Myself and my pal Justin are just hanging out for a bit. You're more than welcome.'

Twenty minutes later, I called down for Martin and Eoin to join us, and soon the five of us were sitting around a stove in the yurt, sharing stories and songs. *This is fantastic. I can't believe it*, I thought, realising that only a few hours before I had been facing the prospect of a lonely wet night on the hill with neither food nor company.

We sat laughing late into the night as Marty and Justin entertained us with exciting tales about the myths and magic of Uisneach. It turned out that the lads were friends of hill custodians David and Angela and ran regular cultural and historic tours there.

'People don't realise how special this place is,' said Justin, who had spent years in the music industry but had recently given it up to focus on his passion for history and archaeology. 'For thousands of years, people have gathered on this hill for feasts and fairs. They came from all over Ireland and shared stories, exchanged ideas and hatched plans. Just like we're doing here tonight, lads!'

———

'Ah, there you are,' said Eoin as I returned from my morning bathroom run. He was in his element, playing king of the campsite as he danced around, cooking up a storm. By the time the hot breakfast was ready, Marty had appeared, and we once again sat in a circle, feasting and joking like men without a care in the world.

Justin had already returned home, but Marty was more than able to fill in when it came to sharing the lore of the hill, with passion and knowledge that seemed limitless. He was infatuated, perhaps in love, with Uisneach, and he wanted the world to know about it.

'Egypt has the pyramids and the Valley of the Kings, and Peru has Machu Picchu and the Sacred Valley. Uisneach, Tara, and the various sites that link to these – this is our equivalent. This heritage is of profound significance,' he told me, throwing his arms into the air in a gesture of pure pride.

'The plan to build industrial-scale turbines nearby could compromise our vision and threaten our hopes of getting UNESCO support for Uisneach, so we need to keep an eye on that. Obviously, a lot of damage was done by the building of the new motorway through the Tara-Skryne valley, but hopefully we can avoid some of it. God knows the midlands has so much to offer, and this is a perfect focal point – and one we should be proud of.'

I felt I could spend a week hanging out and chatting with the lads, but the morning was drifting by. Alas, I would need to keep moving.

Eoin and Martin had offered me a lift back to Cootehill, and it was tempting. I hadn't been to County Cavan during the trip, and it might be possible to swing a quick visit and hitch on to Dublin from there. But all the talk of hills and heritage had also got me thinking of Tara, perhaps Ireland's most famous hill, which was only about half an hour away.

'How about we visit Tara and go for a walk, and I can decide whether or not to go with you to Cootehill or head back to Dublin from there?' I put to the lads.

'Maybe I'll see yis at the Electric Picnic festival in September?' Marty said as we packed our bags and thanked him for his excellent hospitality. 'I help run the MindField area there, and I'll be doing some poetry too, so pop over if you make it along.'

'What, you're a poet?' Eoin asked Marty.

'Well it's more like spoken word, to be honest, but yeah, I do a bit.'

'Go on, recite us a poem, would ya?' Eoin requested, rubbing his hands together exactly as his father, Pete, used to.

Marty looked around sheepishly, as if it was ever in doubt. It was a kind of ritual that Irish people tend to do before offering up a song or a poem. A dance of 'Ah, I dunno, I dunno . . .' met with choruses of 'Go on, aah go on . . .'

'Okay, I will so!' Marty relented before plunging deep into thought. He loosened up his shoulders, fixed his hair and straightened his stance as if to announce something important. The anticipation grew as we sat around the mounds of a ring fort that once formed the perimeter of King Tuathal Teachtmar's Royal Palace back in the first century AD.

Before we knew it, Marty had jumped right into the centre of the enclosure, as though it was a stage upon which he was born to stand. His solemn expression and serious demeanour suggested a depth I hadn't yet detected in this seemingly carefree, fun-loving man. He cleared his throat and began, sharing words that captured so much of what my trip had been about.

> When you feel like you're in the middle of the storm,
> feel like nothing on earth could possibly keep you warm,
> don't think of the rain as depressing,
> it's earth's blessing so life can grow.
> And don't be afraid because the sun will rise tomorrow,
> and believe that you'll find strength in this fight . . .

Marty's poem, entitled 'This Will Pass', carried a raw emotion that reverberated through the sacred site as we joined in applause for our new friend. Our wounds and worries seemed alchemised by the medicinal rhythm of his words; words of hope and of healing.

————

The green fields of Westmeath glistened beneath the tall trees that lined our route into County Meath. I felt a natural high, strengthened by gratitude, as we continued to the Hill of Tara – door-to-door delivery from one ancient royal site to the other.

Something had shifted in me. It was as if the night on Uisneach had been a kind of closing ceremony, a celebration of my trip and all I had experienced. I was feeling excited, confident and upbeat. Anxiety about the Council of State meeting had left me, and I was no longer worried about the future. There were so many challenges to attend to, in my own life and in the world, but I felt a shift in how I could approach them. I was finally learning to surrender, to fully let go and trust in the flow of life a bit more.

Part of me knew I could have done better on this trip – been more adventurous, visited more places, heard more diverse voices. But the unplanned journey had followed its own script, one I was not always in charge of. I had set out on a mission to listen, and for the most part I had given it my all.

What lay ahead, I could not say. Right now, I was being chauffeured to the Hill of Tara, and life was good. I was in the moment and that was all that mattered.

18

Making Hope Happen

The Áras to Glenties

'JUST CHECKING YOU'RE STILL GOOD FOR THAT ARTICLE today? I need it by 4pm at the latest,' messaged the editor from the *Irish Independent*.

'Oh no!' I exclaimed. Between my time with the lads on Uisneach and my decision to visit the Hill of Tara, I had totally forgotten. I now had less than two hours to write an article summarising my trip for a national newspaper. It was a major opportunity to share reflections from the journey, but it meant the trip to Cootehill with Eoin and Martin wouldn't be possible. Disappointed, I explained the situation and thanked the lads for what had been a memorable time together. *Maybe the lads were envoys of sorts*, I thought to myself as I waved good-bye to them – ambassadors from the place that had started me off in the world of hitchhiking all those years ago.

I ventured to Maguire's café at the foot of the Hill of Tara and took out my laptop. With the clock ticking, I took a deep breath and went for it. 'There is hope for Ireland, and I have the evidence,' the article began, as I sought to put words to all I had experienced. 'Ireland is a nation that is re-examining its core values. It is through a return to community that we are reimagining the country from the ground up, finding light in the darkness. There is an emerging return to understanding that true happiness comes from the simple things in life – from friends, family, community, nature and having a purpose bigger than ourselves.'

I clicked *send* just as my deadline arrived and let out a loud 'woo-hoo' in celebration, which prompted several customers to look around with intrigue. I smiled back, a little embarrassed, before laughing to myself. At this stage, I didn't particularly care what anyone thought of me. People would have to take me as they found me, and I would need to start going a little easier on myself too. There was something to be said for being able to shout 'woo-hoo' in public and enjoy it.

––––––

I decided to take a moment and have a last wander around the hill before the final road home. I had no sooner ventured by the Lia Fáil ('stone of destiny') coronation stone at the inauguration mound on Tara than the sky opened up again. What had been weeks of glorious sunshine were now giving way to torrential rain.

'Don't think of the rain as depressing, it's earth's blessing so life can grow.' The words from Marty's poem rang fresh in my head as I looked to the sky and smiled. A blessing the rain might be, but moments later I was drenched to the bone. I decided to run for cover, but hurrying down the hill I slipped in the mud and fell full-on into a puddle.

'Hey buddy, are you okay?' came a voice from nearby. 'Come over here for some shelter.'

I looked over to see two men peering out from beneath a makeshift plastic canopy; yet more mysterious hitching helpers appearing just as I needed them, as if angels were watching over me. I joined the men under their tarp, and we laughed together like children. 'Ah, it's good to be alive, it's good to be alive!' remarked one of the men, before telling me he was visiting Tara for the first time after recently being released from prison.

My new pals suggested I would be best to get a bus back to Dublin given my soaking-wet state. I dearly wanted to hitch, but it was hard to disagree. They offered to drive me to a nearby bus stop, and we departed the Hill of Tara with Tom Petty's 'Free Fallin'' blaring from their van.

'We can't allow you to arrive back to your lady looking worse than you do now,' one of the guys laughed, and in a final gesture of kindness they waited with me for ten minutes for the bus to arrive, so I didn't risk getting any wetter.

An hour later, I had finally warmed up and was starting to drift off to sleep as the bus pulled into Dublin city centre. It was late evening, and the rain had ended, clearing the way for the sun to cast its hazy pinkish light over the River Liffey and the bridges that stretched across it.

Couples walked hand in hand and tourists posed for photographs, while homeless people sat on the pavement staring down on the grey concrete. A man paced up and down O'Connell Street, wearing a sign that advertised a seedy strip club, and evening buses packed with weary workers shuttled past. A group of teenagers ran by, shouting at their friends to hurry up, as a Romanian accordion player offered a tune layered with sadness and possibility.

This was Dublin in all its glory and chaos. Though I had moved here somewhat reluctantly three years previously, I had come to love the place: its raw energy, its edgy and colourful characters, its historical treasures, and the natural beauty of Dublin Bay. It could be tough to appreciate at times – the traffic, poverty, grime and crime overshadowing its kinder features – but at its core Dublin was a charmer, a wild rogue with a soft soul that had captured my heart. Whether Dublin would remain my home for much longer, I still wasn't sure. I had given up thinking about the future and for now, it was good to be back.

'Where are you?' Susan texted not long after I had landed in the city.

'On my way! I can't wait to see you,' I replied as my heart filled with excitement. Susan had been my grounding force, a steady rock of support and wise counsel throughout the trip. She had lovingly encouraged the idea from the onset, as she has done for so many of my ideas and adventures over the years.

'No shackles bind us, we are free together,' goes a line from a song she wrote, capturing our long-standing commitment to grow together while continuing to support each other's freedom to follow our own dreams.

I'm a lucky man, I thought as I arrived back to her warm embrace.

───────

Thousands of pages lay stacked on the kitchen table. I had got a good night's sleep and even managed an early-morning dip in the sea, but the task ahead was slightly intimidating. It was 7am, and I had three full days to prepare for the Monday afternoon Council of State meeting.

The sensitivity of the abortion legislation in question meant the task required the utmost respect. I was not being asked to give my view on abortion or even on the merits of the legislation, since parliament had already passed it, but to establish whether or not it was constitutional. Ultimately, I had to come to my own conclusion and be ready to speak with clarity, confidence and understanding. The Council of State members' collective guidance would help the President decide whether to sign it into law or refer it to the Supreme Court for a final decision.

Referral to the Supreme Court would mean the legislation would no longer be open to challenge. If the court ruled against the bill, it could be years before new legislation was drafted to replace it. If the court ruled in favour of the legislation, its opposers would not have an opportunity to challenge it later.

At nightfall, my head spinning from all I had read and been told by the scholars and experts I'd consulted by phone, I went for a solitary walk on Dollymount Strand to process what I had learned and to pinpoint my own blind spots or biases. I found myself standing under the giant *Realt Na Mara* statue of the Virgin Mary, at the end of the Bull Wall, looking out to sea. As I stood there considering the significance of the question at hand, it became clear to me what I would say at the meeting. I needed to figure out how exactly to say it.

───────

By Monday morning, I was ready. I had prepared for the meeting as best I could, and I reminded myself that I wasn't there to debate or impress.

As I walked past a line of photographers at the entrance of Áras an Uachtaráin, I had to smile to myself at the contrast. Only days before, I'd been lying in the mud on the Hill of Tara, site of the ancient kings, and today I was dressed in my finery at the house of the President, the highest office in modern Ireland.

In the reception room, President Higgins and his wife Sabina stood warmly greeting guests. I prepared to shake his hand, but he caught me off guard and pulled me in for a hug that immediately eased any lingering nerves. 'I hear you've been touring the country, Ruairí,' the President said.

'Well, I was, until a couple of days ago, but duty called, President, so here I am,' I replied. 'I look forward to telling you all about it when the dust settles.'

The gathering felt slightly surreal. Most of the faces were recognisable because they had been major figures in Irish life over the decades: An Taoiseach (Prime Minister) Enda Kenny, An Tánaiste (Deputy Prime Minister) Joan Burton, former president Mary McAleese, former Taoisigh John Bruton and Brian Cowen, and others.

Towards the large windows at the back of the room, I spotted Catherine McGuinness, Sally Mulready, Gerard Quinn, Michael Farrell, Gearóid Ó Tuathaigh and Deirdre Heenan, who made up the other six of the President's seven appointees to the Council of State. Since our inauguration gathering we had crossed paths at various events, including the annual Easter Rising commemorations at Dublin's General Post Office and at Arbour Hill.

This is all a bit mad, I thought to myself before being directed into the State Reception Room where Council of State members were being asked to pose for media photographers.

'Mr McKiernan, could you come over here, please?' signalled the photographer, pointing towards former Taoiseach Brian Cowen, who succeeded Bertie Ahern after he resigned in 2008 in the wake of revelations at the Mahon corruption tribunal. This was starting to feel a bit ridiculous. After all the stories I had heard on the road, I had so much I wanted to say to these men – so many questions to ask. It was Brian Cowen who had signed off on the 2008 bank guarantee – one of the world's biggest banking bailouts – which saddled tiny Ireland with 42 per cent of the EU's banking debt, a decision that would hit us hard for decades to come.

'Okay everyone, smile for the camera please,' came the call from the photographer, thereby ending my musings about the politicians beside me. Soon after we were called into the Council of State room, where the President reminded us that the proceedings were confidential.

The meeting was over in a matter of hours; it had come and gone in a flash. We had shared our views on the historic legislation with the President, and the final decision was his. I lingered for a while afterwards, thinking about the magnitude of the day and the families of Savita Halappanavar and so many others affected by these issues. I hoped that the final outcome might offer them some solace and prevent future suffering.

It was almost 8pm, and I needed to get going. I was due to speak at the MacGill conference in County Donegal the next morning and still hadn't prepared for my address. There was no time to delay. I met Susan at the gates of Áras an Uachtaráin, and we hit the road to Donegal, arriving into the sleepy village of Glenties after midnight.

Here I was at the very end of the line, for the speaking engagement that had first sparked the idea for my trip.

———

I arose at 6am with just hours to prepare.

'I'll make you breakfast, and you focus on your talk,' Susan offered with her usual kindness and care. By 10am, I had prepared notes and done two radio interviews. I was still processing my experiences and wasn't sure how I could possibly do justice to all the people and stories I had encountered along the way. The Council of State meeting had left me feeling a little scattered, but if there was one thing I had learned, it was to keep breathing and trust that the path would unfold before me.

On the main street, we bumped into Joe Mulholland, the driving force behind MacGill. 'Ah, the rambler has arrived,' Joe teased with a wide smile as he welcomed us into the venue and explained, providing much relief, that my talk had been postponed until after lunch. The universe had granted the extra hours needed to gather myself.

When the time finally came and broadcaster Seán O'Rourke called me to the stage, I took a deep breath and launched into a reflection of the trip and some of the stories I had heard on the road. I spoke about the angst and frustration I had felt prior to setting out – that like so many, I had been struggling to maintain a sense of hope for the future. I shared how the journey had felt like a leap of faith, how I began with no money and no plan, and how right from the beginning people had got behind me. I told the stories of the people of Oughterard and Inishbofin, the farmers in Maam, my trip to Croagh Patrick and my adventures with the Italian tourists in County Mayo. I relayed that while many of the people I had encountered were angry and indignant, I had also discovered a sense of community spirit that was still very much alive, and very much holding the country together.

I told the packed room about the visit with my grandmother and my friend Keith in Donegal, the excursion to Larry's farm, and my unforgettable experience in Derry. I recounted my memories of the wedding in County Kildare, the people I met around the streets of Dublin, of Paul and James in Aughrim, and Colm, Caroline and Jane in County Wexford. I wanted to impart the sense of liberation I had felt from day one. I wanted the audience to feel the generosity of those who offered lifts, money, food, beds and most important, their stories. Stories of struggle and stress, of hardship and holding on, and stories of standing up, speaking out and creating change in ways both obvious and subtle. I wanted them to feel that sense of connection I felt in the field in Dunmore East, and to hear the voices of people like Sarah in Cork, who had been through so much but was determined to fight for a better way. I reflected on the dedication of the community workers in Limerick, and that magical night of camping on the Hill of Uisneach. It was a story of community, of soul-searching, simplicity and learning to let go.

My talk might not have been too well planned, but standing there addressing that crowd, I opened my heart so that they might see what I had seen – the heart and soul of Ireland. A heart filled with hurt and sadness yet beating strong and proud and filled with dreams and possibilities.

As I returned to my seat, a man approached and tapped me on the back.

'Excuse me, I don't want to interrupt, but I just heard your talk and wanted to give you this,' he said, slipping something into my hand as he shook it. Before I knew it, he was gone, leaving me with €100 in cash – money that was much needed for the bills that hadn't disappeared while I was on the road. The trip might have ended, but the goodwill kept coming.

———

Just as my thoughts turned to home, the phone rang to introduce one final challenge before I could end the adventure. It was a researcher from RTÉ Radio 1 wanting to know if I'd come on its flagship Marian Finucane show the next morning in Dublin. Broadcaster Áine Lawlor was filling in for Marian and was keen to have me on.

At this stage, I felt completely spent and had no desire to do any more talking. Yet this was a golden opportunity to use my platform by speaking to the nation on one of the country's most-listened-to radio shows. We left Glenties at 6am and arrived at RTÉ with minutes to spare after getting lost on one-way streets in Dublin's south side.

In the RTÉ waiting room, I met writer and filmmaker Ferdia MacAnna and his friend, the author and agent Vanessa O'Loughlin. 'That trips sounds amazing,' Ferdia said.

'Maybe you'll write a book about it someday,' Vanessa added.

'I very much doubt that,' I replied. 'I think this is the end of it now.' Little did I know.

The broadcast began, and Áine asked me her first question: 'You had your first Council of State meeting – tell me, was it intimidating?'

I went to speak, but nothing would come out. *Oh no*, I thought. *This is a total disaster*. Tiredness had set in, and I was losing my voice. After a slight panic, I paused and focused on my breathing. Years of meditation practice was coming in handy. I tried again, and I was off. I found my groove in what was to be an enjoyable interview, helped by Áine's frindly demeanour.

'Were there any particular encounters that stand out for you?' Áine wanted to know.

I thought for a second. There had been so many people, so many stories, and it seemed impossible to highlight any particular one over the other. So much of what had transpired in my own thoughts was subtle. Experiences and insights had worked their way gently into my system and were still churning.

Then a voice came into my head: *The wolves ... tell her about the wolves.*

It was the perfect moment to share the story relayed to me by a young Polish immigrant to Ireland who thought she didn't have much to contribute; a story from a culture that wasn't her own, and yet offered universal wisdom.

I told Áine and the listeners the Native American tale of the two wolves fighting for control of our minds – the wolf of greed, envy, hate and fear against the wolf of kindness, compassion, hope and love. I recalled the young woman's beautiful storytelling, and how she brought the tale to a close with the grandchild worriedly asking his grandparent, 'And which wolf will win?' The grandparent replies: 'The one that will win is the one that you feed.'

Perhaps the story sounded a little strange to the more hardened hearts of a nation beset by economic and political woe. After all, I could see why people might resist a self-help sensibility when so much structural and systemic change is needed. Yet my experience on the road had shown me that in fostering hope, both matter – the personal and the political – and that the personal shapes the political through an interconnected web of change. We could choose to be victims in this, or to rise up as warriors and weavers of a new reality.

Epilogue

I BELIEVE MY HITCHING FOR HOPE LISTENING TOUR offers a modest example of how new roads exist if we are curious enough to go looking for them. It has instigated many unexpected ripples of change throughout my life; it's brought me the opportunity to travel around Ireland and internationally, giving talks and workshops; it led me to create the *Love and Courage* podcast; and, of course, it gave way to this book. It also opened up new and enriching friendships, and most importantly, it reminded me that there is always hope for humanity, as long as we remember that hope doesn't just happen, we need to get out there and make it happen. 'Action breeds hope.'

Reflecting on all this after the trip, the idea of emigration no longer seemed appealing. I had fallen in love with Ireland again and was ready to stay, to serve and to contribute, regardless of what challenges lay ahead. I was now ready to build my life in Ireland with my beautiful wife-to-be and to create new adventures together with her.

That my trip lasted only a month is proof that life-changing experiences don't need to take years or cost the earth. I truly believe that profound adventures await us if we find the courage to answer the call to action by leaping into the unknown.

In a world facing irreversible ecological collapse, massive inequality and loud voices of division, this call is ever urgent. How can we create and maintain hope when faced with often overwhelming obstacles? That's a question to be answered by people like you and me, in how we choose to respond to the challenges of our time. We can go down a road either of fear or of love; we either stand by or stand up.

The road ahead will look different for each of us, but it's easier to navigate our unique twists and turns when we support one another – when we're not afraid to stick out our thumbs and ask for help. None of us can do it alone. Whatever your call to adventure looks like, I write these words with the wish that your journey is a great one. As the old Irish blessing goes, *Go n-éirí an bóthar leat*: 'may the road rise to meet you.'

ACKNOWLEDGEMENTS

The Hitching for Hope listening tour, this book, the *Love and Courage* podcast and my various other projects would not be possible without the support of family, friends and a wide circle of community. For this, I feel tremendous gratitude. I want to express my heartfelt thanks to my beloved wife Susan, who is a constant source of love, support and inspiration. Thanks also to my parents, my brother and sister, my relatives, in-laws and all my friends, allies, teachers and mentors. Huge thanks to all who shared their story with me, to those in the media who have helped, and to anyone who donated online, gave me lifts, places to stay, food to eat, spaces to work, and offered advice and encouragement along the way. A big thanks to all the wonderful team at Chelsea Green who are a joy to work with, especially Natalie Wallace. My sincerest thanks to Sarah Ingle, Doreen Martens, Simon Ward, Niamh Devereux, Ronan Carroll, Marie Duffy and Jodi Henderson for going above and beyond, and also to Eamon Stack from Enclude and Joe Murray from Afri for ongoing support. My love and thanks to all in the wider tribe that has held, supported and inspired me in various ways, seen and unseen, including those listed here and those I may have inadvertently omitted (please forgive me): Ada Broek, Adrian Herlihy, Adrian Ryan, Aidan Cronin, Aidan Gordon, Áine Coughlan, Áine Lawlor, Áine Lennon, Alan Gielty, Alan Gilsenan, Alan Quigley, Alex Foster, Alice Kennelly, Alison Oldfield, Allen Meagher, Allyson Lambert, Andrew Gibbons, Andrew Madden, Angela Dorgan, Ann Keenaghan, Anna Coyle, Anne Sheridan, Anne Symens-Bucher, Aonghus Sammin, Aoife Woodlock, Avril Stanley, Barry Dillon, BBC Radio Foyle *Mark Patterson Show* team, Ben Brandzel, Bertie and Mairéad

Quirke, Bill McKibben, Brandy McDonagh, Breezy Kelly, Breffni Clarke, Brenda Coulter, Brendan Kennedy, Brian O'Connell, Brian Reynolds, Bróna Moriarty, Caitriona Quirke and Vincent, James, Hannah and Rosie Downes, Candice Moen, Carla McNeil, Caroline Crowley and family, Caroline McGuigan, Caroline Price, Cathal Ó Gabhann, Celia Keenaghan, Charles Shovlin, Charlie Ryder, Christopher Keenaghan, Christina Butt, Christy Moore, Chuck Collins, Claire Hayes, Claire Kiernan, Clare Herbert, Colleen Barry, Colm Mac Con Iomaire, Colm O'Snodaigh, Colm Quearney, Colman Farrell, Colum McCann, Colum Stapleton, Conor Hickey, Conor McKay, Coralie Mureau, Damien Mulley, Dan Keenaghan (RIP), Dan O'Neill, Daniel Keenaghan and family, Danny Cusack, Danny Daly, Danny Forde, Danny Murray, Dara Twamley, Darragh Doyle, Darragh Keenaghan, Darren Ryan, Dave Cunningham, Dave Curran, Dave Donnellan, Dave Lordan, David and Angela Clarke, David Laurence Quinn, David Patterson, Davin Roche, Davy Ward, Dean Scurry, Dearbhail McDonald, Deborah Erwin, Deborah Molloy, Declan Heeney and Simon Hess at Gill Hess, Deirdre Cole and Samuel Ponnuthurai, Deirdre Garvey, Deirdre Ní Chinnéide, Deirdre Mortell, Dermot Curristin, Derry O'Donnell, Des Moran, Dessie Farrell, Diarmuid Lyng, Dieter Gerhardt, Dil Wickremasinghe, Dolores Whelan, Dónal O'Kelly, Dublin Occupy Love, Eamonn Callaghan, Eddie Neville, Eileen Cameron, Eileen Mulcahy, Eithne McAdam, Elaine McCabe, Eliza Haun, Ellen Mayns, Emma Cosgrove, Enda Donnellan, Enda Reilly, Eoin McHugh, Eoin Ó Broin, Eoin Ward, Eugene Claffey, Fenella Fay and family, Fiach Mac Conghail, Fiachna Ó Braonáin, Fiona Ó hAodha, Flor Sylvester, Fr. Séamus Whitney, Frances Black, Frances Byrne, Galway girl, Gary and Linnea Dunne, Gavin Clarke, Geraldine Keane, Grace Dyas, Grace Gerry, Graham Merrigan, Heather Gray, Helen Henderson, Hugh O'Brien, Hugh O'Reilly, Ian McGahon, Ina O'Murchu, Jackie McKiernan, Jackie McQuillan, Jacqui Corcoran, James Connolly, James O'Dea, James O'Sullivan, Jane Ann O'Connell, Jane Forman, Jane Johnstone, Janet Gaynor, Jen Rice, Jenna Cosgrove, Jenna Stewart, Jennifer Moroney-Ward, Jill Kiedaisch, Jim Cotter, Jim McKiernan (RIP), Jim Patten, Jimmy D'Arcy, Jimmy Davis, Joanna Heffernan,

ACKNOWLEDGEMENTS

Joanna Macy, Joe Dower and friends, Joe Flynn, Joe Mullholland and the MacGill team, Joseph Keenaghan, John and Jacqueline Keenaghan, John Cantwell, John Concannon, John Dawson, John Evoy, John Hession, John Higgins, John Kenny, John Joe Lennon, John Lillis, John Maguire, John McColgan, Jon Rae, Jonathan Lee Newell, Jonathan Woods, Joseph Kavanagh, Justin Moore and family, Kahlil Coyle, Kalle Ryan, Karen Furlong, Karen Henshaw, Karen Ward, Kate Lawlor, Kate O'Halloran, Kathryn McKiernan, Kathy Scott, Katie Read, Kees Duson, Keith Corcoran, Keith Kelly, Keith Moore, Ken King, Kiernan Clifford, Kingsley Aikins, Kurt Nikolaisen, Larry Masterson, Larry O'Connell, Larry Reynolds, Laura Murphy, Laura Nulty, Laura Power, Liam Collins, Limerick Learning Hub, Lisa Consiglio and all at Narrative 4, Lisa Nic an Bhreithimh, Lisa Patten, Lisa Tierney-Keogh, Lizbeth Goodman, Lorcan Mulhern, Lorna Siggins, Lorraine McMullen, Louise Heneghan, Luke Concannon, Lydia Kiernan, Lynn Boylan, Luka Bloom, Mano Ponnuthurai, Máire Uí Eidhin, Mairéad Brady, Mairéad Ní Chaoimh, Máirín Connolly, Maisie and James McKiernan (RIP), Malachy Moynihan, Marco Capuano and Simona Poce, Marcus Magee, Margaret Dorgan, Margo Baldwin, Mari Kennedy, Marian Keyes, Marie and Barry Dempsey, Marie Coyne, Marie Molloy, Marie Therese Power, Martin Lennon, Martin McBennett, Marty Mulligan, Mary Atkinson, Mary Brennan, Mary Cunningham, Mary Hawkes, Mary Elizabeth Keenaghan, Mary Keenaghan, Mary Wallace Collins, Matt Haslum, Meadhbh Cleary, Megan Brown, Michael Birt, Michael Gibbons, Michael McArdle, Michael McCaughan, Michael McDonnell, Michael Metivier, Micheál O'Ciardubháin, Michael Weaver, Michelle Gannon, Miffy Hoad, Molly Rowan Leach, Muireannn De Barra, Naomi Linehan, Natalie Wallace, Niall Doherty, Niall Ó'Faoláin, Niall Whelan, Niamh Gunn, Niamh Ní Chonchubhair, Nóirín Ní Riain, Noreen Neary, Norma Smurfit, Nuala Kavanagh, Olive Towey, Órla de Búrca, Orlagh O'Brien, Owen Keenan, PJ Fitzgerald, PJ O'Reilly, Paddy Duffy, Padraic O'Brien, Pat Ryan, Patrice Reilly, Patrick Cusack, Pati Stone, Patti McCann, Pauhla McGrane, Paul Byrne, Paul Gogarty, Paul McKiernan, Paul Stassen, Pearse McGloughlin, Peggy Seeger, Peter Daly, Peter Lynn, President Michael D. Higgins,

Sabina and all the staff at the Áras, Rachel Sherlock, Ray Magee, Ray McCaul, Ray Nangle Sr., Rebecca Dunne, Rebecca Thorn, Richard Boyle, Richard Lawson, Rita Minehan, Rob Davey, Rodney Lancashire, Róisín, Hannah and Paula McGrogan, RoJ Whelan, Ron Hulshof, Ronan Branigan, Ronan Cosgrove, Ronan Lehane, Rosaleen Callaghan, Rose Baldwin, Ross Fitzpatrick, Ruairí McCaul, Ruth Maher, Ruth O'Mahony and Simon Brown, Sandra J. Clifford, Sandra O'Reilly, Sandy and Steven McKiernan, Sara Burke, Sarah Clancy, Sarah Kovach, Sarah Lyons, Sarah Martin, Sarah McEneaney, Seán Boland, Seán Coughlan, Seán Gray, Seán Maher, Seán McKiernan, Seán O'Rourke Jr., Seán Óg, Rosemary, and Róisín McKiernan, Sheamus O'Reilly, Sinéad Hession, Sinéad McKiernan and Barry Healy, Sinéad Troy, Sinéad Garvey and all at the Cheese Press, Siobhán Earley, Siobhán O'Donoghue, Sonia Semchechen, Sophia Duffy, Sr. Majella McCarron, Stephen Cawley, Stephan James Smith, Stephen Kelleher, Sunny and Peter at the Sunny Center, Susan Megy, Suzanne Sheils, Suzanne Zanchetta, Tanya Ward, Tarinna Terrel, Tim Hourigan, Timothy O'Donoghue, Tomás Hardinian, Tommy Graham, Tony Bates, Tony Griffin, Tony O'Brien, Treacy O'Connor, Trevor White, Ultan McNasser, Vanessa O'Loughlin, Vasile Bria, Veronika Stalder, Victoria Nash and Wesley Dunne. Thanks also to the staff of the various places I have worked on this book including Raheny Library, Glenstal Monastery, Javaholics in Fairview, Slí an Chroí in County Wicklow, Clontarf Castle, the Armada Hotel, Atlantic Hotel in Lahinch, the Falls Hotel and Byrne's Townhouse in Ennistymon, Hugo's Deli in Lahinch and the Rock Shop in Liscannor. To anyone I left out, please let me know so I can make it up to you. My love and gratitude to each and all.

INDEX

INDEX

ABOUT THE AUTHOR

ALEX FOSTER

RUAIRÍ McKIERNAN is an award-winning social innovator, campaigner and charity founder. He is a Fulbright scholar, a former Presidential appointee to Ireland's Council of State, and a regular media contributor on social, environmental and health issues. Ruairí hosts the popular *Love and Courage* podcast, which features inspirational voices for change from around the world. He travels throughout Ireland and abroad offering talks, workshops, retreats, consultancy, mentoring and campaigning support to individuals and organisations working for change. Ruairí lives on the west coast of County Clare with his wife, Susan Quirke, who is a singer, songwriter, musician and meditation teacher.

For more information on Ruairí and to find photos, videos and audio related to this book, please visit: www.ruairimckiernan.com.

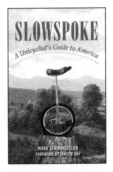

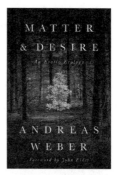
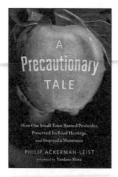
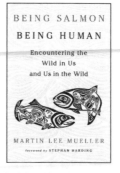